From Pain
To Peace

Pat Bluth

AXIOM
PRESS

Mobile, Alabama

From Pain To Peace
by Pat Bluth
Copyright ©2008 Pat Bluth

ISBN 978-1-58169-295-2
For Worldwide Distribution
Printed in the U.S.A.

Axiom Press
P.O. Box 191540 • Mobile, AL 36619
800-367-8203

Editor's Note:
Only first names are used in this book
to protect the privacy of those involved.

Dedication

To my family:
my husband, Gary;
our daughter, Jennifer;
our son, Jeff, and our daughter-in-law, Tracy;
and to my three grandchildren:
Karlee, Alexa and Jackson.
I thank God you are in my life.

This book is written in loving memory of my daughter, Tammy, born October 19th, 1967, and killed September 13th, 1985, the victim of a drunk driver.

My prayer is that this book will provide inspiration and encouragement to all those who grieve, and especially to those who feel unable to forgive.

May this book help show how to let go of anger and bitterness, and find peace and forgiveness.

This is my story of grief and how God saved my life by showing me that forgiveness is the only way to healing and lasting peace.

Table of Contents

Acknowledgments

So many people played an important role in the completion of this book. Without their help and encouragement it may never have been written.

Gary, my dear husband, you were there with me every step of the way. Your patience and love sustained me. Jennifer and Jeff, my children, supported me in telling our family story so others might benefit.

As I became involved with grief groups, I learned that everyone grieves differently, each having a unique journey toward healing. Those who attended the groups I facilitated taught me this, and their open sharing of their pain reminded me I was not alone. My prayer is that they will continue to heal and find the peace and serenity they so deeply deserve.

What would I have done without my friends? Mary, Mary Claire, my Cursillo support group: you listened; you cried with me; you truly cared; and most importantly, you prayed and prayed and prayed. And Loren, Kathy, Karen, and Mary, you were among those who stepped forward to encourage me to share my story in book form, and you and others were there to support me along the way. The word "thanks" simply doesn't suffice.

The Compassionate Friends group was just what they claimed to be: loving and caring brothers and sisters who shared pain and sorrow and gave me hope that survival was possible.

During this time my faith was challenged, yes, but God was there to hear my cries. He sent His servants to help me see how He had not forsaken me. Among those servants were Father Con, who encouraged me to attend the Loyola Silent Retreat. There, Brother Bill and other staff listened and provided guidance. Father Greg, my spiritual director, has remained a constant rock in hard times, always helping bring me back to the Lord when I begin to drift away.

I want to thank Mothers Against Drunk Driving, MADD. This organization with national, state and local offices have educated me and provided me with many invaluable resources. As an active member of this organization, I have made many friends and have found an outlet for my anger and a means to help others who have been devastated by drunk driving.

Dorrie O'Brien, my editor, has been so supportive and kept encouraging me all along the way. Her advice and suggestions have been much appreciated and have made for a better book. She believed in me and was able to edit my writing and not change the essence of what I had written. Thank you, Dorrie.

Thank you to Guy Doud for writing such an inspirational foreword. Your ongoing encouragement throughout the writing process has been deeply appreciated.

And to all those I was not able to include here: You all have a special place in my heart. My most sincere thanks and appreciation.

Foreword

On a Friday in September of 1985, Tammy Bluth was a beautiful senior girl who sat toward the front in my discussion class at Brainerd High School in Brainerd, Minnesota. She was full of life and fun. She had a marvelous sense of humor and a great outlook on life. It was obvious she was "going places."

The following Monday, our entire class sat in shocked grief trying to deal with the details of Tammy's death. On Friday night, after the football game, she had been killed by a drunken driver. Now, over 20 years later, I must admit that I could have been that driver.

In this book, Tammy's mother, Pat, shares her story, from the moment she hears of Tammy's death, to the long process involved in her grief-recovery. It is a story of a journey—long and hard. It is a story of courage, of doubt and faith, of anger and rage—understandable anger and rage. Ultimately, it is a story of hope and forgiveness that will touch any reader on numerous levels.

From Pain To Peace, however, is also a call for continued reform of our nation's drunken driving laws. Too many people, often thinking they are not impaired, and some who know that they are, climb behind the wheels of vehicles. These vehicles become lethal weapons. Despite millions of dollars spent on anti-drinking and driving campaigns, many people still haven't gotten the message: it is never okay to drink and drive. I was one of those people. It took a DWI arrest for me to finally admit that I had taken other's lives into my hands, when I got behind the wheel, after having drinks with friends at my favorite neighborhood bar. I take little solace in a recent survey where over 30% of Minnesotans acknowledge driving under the influence at one time or another. This behavior must end. The truth is: I could have killed someone.

Pat Bluth was instrumental in starting the MADD (Mother's Against Drunk Driving) chapter in our area. I've actually heard people ridicule and curse this organization: "MADD is ruining all our fun!" Of course, these are people who have never lost a child to some drunk behind the wheel.

Perhaps the content of this book sounds a little heavy and depressing; however, it is anything but. It is a marvelous story of how love and forgiveness can conquer and win over bitterness and rage. It is a story of how God can bring healing to our deepest hurts. It is a reminder of the simple things in life and how to appreciate them. Pat shares her journey, and the accounts of her spiritual retreats provide a model that all of us can find useful. Oh, the power of silence, alone, apart from this hectic and loud world, finally able to hear the voice of God!

This is a book I wish all parents could read. We all think that our children will outlive us. That's the way it is supposed to be. Pat's story reminds us that every day of life is a gift from God and we must never take life for granted.

It is a book I wish all couples could read—especially couples who have encountered tragedy in their families. Pat's husband, Gary, handled his grief so differently from Pat, and this sharp contrast could have ended their marriage, if there hadn't been commitment and understanding.

This book should be required reading for all those who insist on drinking and driving. I thank God that those days are behind me and that I never hurt anyone, and that I never will. I pray that stories like Pat's will find an audience who will have open ears to hear, minds to understand, and hearts to act accordingly. Everyone will find some gem from this book to store in their hearts.

—*Guy R. Doud, 1985 Minnesota Teacher of the Year,*
1986 National Teacher of the Year

Chapter 1

Tragedy Hits

Back in 1985, mornings were often complete chaos before everybody left the house, with my husband, Gary, getting ready for his day's work, and our three children—Tammy, a high-school senior; Jeff, a sophomore; and Jennifer, a sixth-grader—getting ready for school. Usually by 7:45 a.m., I had time to enjoy a cup of coffee before beginning my day's commitments.

We were all scheduled to attend the high school football game, the Brainerd, Minnesota team against the Willmar, Minnesota team on Friday the 13th of that September evening. As we finished dinner together, Jeff said he wanted to go to the game with his friend, Mike F., who'd just received his driver's license and was driving their family car alone for the first time. My husband and I weren't so wild about the idea, but Tammy acted as advocate for her brother and helped him negotiate an extended curfew after convincing us to agree to let him go with his friend.

Later, Tammy sat cross-legged on the couch, studying a school book while waiting for her date, Mike M., to show up. Standing only five-foot-four, Tammy was a slim, beautiful, bright, 17-year-old brunette. Not one to waste time, she was involved in basketball, band, choir, and student council. When she did find spare time during the day, she'd usually curl up in a chair or on the couch and read a book.

1

I left for the football game, saying, "See you later."

The unbeaten Brainerd Warriors played and beat the Willmar Cardinals 12-7 to gain their third straight victory. It was an unusually warm September evening, so the stands were filled with cheering supporters. There was a lot of excitement that night because it was such a close game. Willmar had a chance to score in the last minutes but came up short. Brainerd supplied the crucial plays when they most needed them.

After the football game, Gary and I found Tammy and her friend, Mike, and we spent a few minutes talking to them. Jennifer planned to meet us at the car; she'd been sitting with her friends. Tammy introduced us to Mike and said they would be going to the dance at the high school. He was friendly, cordial, and seemed calm about meeting Tammy's parents for the first time. The short visit with them was not enough to get a sense of what Mike was like except to say that I was comfortable with him as Tammy's date for the evening. This was only their second date. Earlier that day Tammy had received a dozen red roses from him. She was excited about the gift, but she did say she hoped the roses weren't meant to express an expectation for her to make a commitment to be Mike's girlfriend. As their relationship was just beginning, she was not ready for that yet.

After arriving home after the game, Gary, Jennifer, and I talked about the evening. How exciting it was to have the best football team! Gary liked reliving each play and kept going over some of the most exciting moments. We asked Jennifer if she'd seen the game or just goofed around with her friends—as a sixth-grader, we were sure the latter was going to be the case. She said she was glad the Warriors won but didn't care much about the details of the game. Jennifer had spotted Tammy and Mike in the bleachers, so she got a glimpse of Mike from a distance. This pleased her, as she had been curious about him and what he looked like. We finally all stopped discussing the game, and Jennifer went off to bed. I went to my bedroom too.

As I was getting ready to sleep, I heard sirens ululating in the distance. I walked to the window and looked out into the darkness, the thought crossing my mind that something might've happened to Jeff and Mike F.

The doorbell rang a short while after at 10:40 p.m. Gary answered it. It was Terry and his wife, Cindy. Terry worked for North Ambulance and had come to tell us he had bad news about our daughter. She had died, he told Gary, in a car accident.

Gary, in a state of shock, came to the bedroom and said, "There's been a terrible car accident, and Tammy has died."

I listened in stunned, unbelieving silence.

No one could have prepared me for the knock on the door, giving me the devastating news about the death of my child. I came out of the bedroom into the dining room where everyone was standing, bewildered, in disbelief, and unable to grasp any facts.

About 10:00 that evening, Tammy, Mike, and Chris (another friend of Tammy's) had been on their way to pick up Chris's boyfriend, who was getting off work at Hasse's Restaurant. Mike was driving a Ford Mustang, and Tammy was sitting in the middle of the front seat with no seatbelt. Chris was sitting to the right of her in the front seat. The car stopped on the highway with its left signal light blinking, waiting for an oncoming car to pass so they could turn left. Even though it was dark, any car driving down the highway could see that their car was stopped.

As they waited to turn left, a speeding car came up behind them and smashed into the rear of the Mustang. Mike said he never saw the car. Perhaps the car did not have its lights on. Because Tammy was sitting in the middle of bucket seats, the impact of the crash threw her into the back seat. The gas tank exploded, and the back seat of the car as well as Tammy were engulfed in flames. Tammy's death certificate says she died of fourth-degree burns. Mike and Chris were saved from death because they were thrown clear of the car. Mike was taken to the hospital where he remained overnight for observation. Chris was taken by ambulance to St. Paul Ramsey Burn Unit, where she remained for over three weeks. She has burns on her hands and ear. She would have extensive surgeries on her hands over the next year.

The driver of the car that caused the crash was taken to the hospital and released that night.

Only an hour earlier, my husband and I had talked to Tammy. How could she be dead?

When I heard the news that my daughter had died, I became hysterical, emitting a gut-wrenching scream. My first thought was to go to her, but I did not know where she was. I fell sobbing into my husband's arms. I could not believe what I had just been told. I did not want to believe that my daughter was dead. Only an hour ago, I had talked to her and said, "I'll see you later." That was the last conversation we would ever have. Death was not supposed to happen to my family. I could not conceive of Tammy dying in a car crash. In the past, of course, a tragedy like this had always happened to another family. But not this time.

The rest of what happened after those first moments is a blur. The tears and pain were too much. I both wanted and did not want to hear more about what happened, but I realized it was too soon—too soon to absorb any more details. *Just let me be for a while,* I thought. I needed to try to gain some composure. It was not possible. Whom should we call first? We had to make an awful decision. Who else would need to hear the news that their granddaughter, niece, sister, or friend had just died? At a time when I was least capable of making decisions, I was forced to make many.

At the same time the emergency personnel delivered the news regarding Tammy, Jeff arrived home safely. I wonder what Jeff thought when he came home and saw the ambulance in the driveway. After hearing from Gary that Tammy had died, Jeff and Jennifer started crying. They needed comfort, but I could not give them any. I remember all of us were in tears. We didn't know where to turn next or what to say. This was just too much. I wanted the whole evening to start over. I wanted to hear something different. Many jumbled thoughts crowded my mind. *I need to go to Tammy. Where is she? How did this happen? What should I do for my other children?* There were too many questions and no answers.

We simply clung to each other in tears.

The world had suddenly become insecure; I'd lost the security I'd had that I was living in a safe world. If death could come to Tammy so suddenly, it could come that quickly for any of us.

Chapter 2

Family Is Precious

Family is the backbone of life. I learned the importance of family when I was growing up in Minnesota on Lake Osakis. I lived on a resort several miles from anyone else, which made me rely on my brothers and sisters for playmates and soul mates. As kids, we did everything together: playing, working, and of course, acting out our sibling rivalry too. We all had to get imaginative when it came to finding things to do. There were no horses to ride on the resort, but we had pigs, so my brothers and I took to riding them instead. My dad didn't like that too much, but we all thought it was great fun. There was little I could not do as a kid. I spent hours every day by the lakeshore fishing, swimming, or visiting with the guests.

I learned responsibility during the summer months at our family-owned resort. When other kids were swimming or fishing, I was cleaning cabins, selling groceries, or serving my mom's hamburgers to our guests. She was a great cook! People came from miles around just to eat her chow mein.

The only time I remember getting into much trouble as a kid was when my siblings were playing house in the barn and started a fire. The weather was cold, and we were trying to stay warm. Memory of the spanking I received still lingers in my mind, but that was the only one I can remember.

I began school at the age of five in a one-room schoolhouse a couple of miles down the road from my house. I didn't have the luxury of riding a school bus; my mode of transportation was my feet. Because my siblings and I found so many things to do along the road on the way home, we probably set records for the longest time to walk two miles because we were so busy picking up bugs and animals and chasing each other or our neighbors. It was also fun to stop at the neighbors' for cookies instead of hurrying home. I'd also often stop along the river and play in the water. My friends and I found many mischievous things to do rather than walk straight home.

Minnesota winters can be very long and cold, even brutal, so my classmates and I learned to be creative during the winter months. We built snow forts at school during recess, for instance. When the teachers called us back, we couldn't even hear the bell. I looked forward to ice fishing during those cold, wintry days. I didn't care if I caught a fish or not; it was just fun being out on the frozen lake with the other kids.

When I was entering seventh grade, my family sold the resort and moved 10 miles away to Long Prairie, where I graduated from high school. Long Prairie only consisted of about 3,000 people at the time, but I felt as if I'd moved to a big city. My graduating class had only 89 students, though, so that was not really the case.

It didn't take us long to meet the neighbor kids after we'd settled in our new home. I spent most evenings playing "Kick the Can," "Annie, Annie, Over," or a wild game of tag.

Since I didn't know what I wanted to be when I grew up, after I graduated from high school, I moved to Minneapolis. I shared an apartment with several high school friends and worked at an insurance company, but that job wasn't what I ultimately wanted to do with my life. Clearly, I needed to get further education, so that spring I enrolled at Bemidji State University. In the early 60s, the only career choices for women were to be teachers, nurses, or secretaries. I began in the secretarial program, but later pursued a degree in teaching. I earned a Bachelor of Science degree in Business Education three years later.

During my senior year in college, I met Gary Bluth, my future husband, on a blind date. Thirty-three years later we say our relationship began as a blind date and has been blind ever since! I could also say I received my "Mrs." degree at college; Gary and I married while he was still in school, majoring in accounting. Gary had begun college right out of high school but took fishing and duck hunting more seriously than studying. Rather than flunk out of college, he dropped out and joined the United States Army. He served three years in Munich, Germany, after taking basic training at Fort Carson, Colorado. He also received schooling at Fort Knox, Kentucky, and Fort Sam Houston in San Antonio, Texas. He has often said that joining the army was the best decision he could have made. He matured as a result of being in the army. His experience helped him become a very responsible husband, father, and businessman. After his discharge, Gary enrolled at Bemidji State University.

It was at Bemidji State that I was first introduced to faith. Faith and spirituality were not a natural part of my childhood. I do not recall any one time when our family went to church together. Spirituality, faith, and God were far from my everyday life. As a child, I never thought about the fact that other families spent time together in church, but ours did not. In fact, it was normal for our family not to get ready for church or Sunday school on Sunday mornings. It just was not part of what we did. My mom and dad believed in God and Jesus but did not take an active part in church activities.

Ironically, we always lived close to a church, but all I ever saw of it was the outside. There was a church down the street just a half-mile from our resort where I went to vacation Bible school for a few years, but two weeks was not long enough to grasp the meaning of Jesus.

Family Is Precious

When I was in college, my roommate would get up and go to church most Sundays. I thought of her as being quite religious because she went to church once a week. She would invite me to go with her, and once in a while I did go, but I found it uncomfortable attending church because of my background. As a young adult, I didn't want anyone to know that I knew nothing about Jesus or what was being talked about in church. As I reflect on my spiritual journey, however, the little seeds that were planted along the way did eventually sprout and blossom.

Gary was a Catholic and attended church every Sunday. It was not unusual to see his dad praying the rosary or reading Scripture. I found that unusual but did not share my thoughts about it. When Gary and I decided to get married, I attended classes with the priest and became a Catholic. It was not something I had to do, but it seemed like a good idea. Since I had no church of my own, I thought it would be easier if I attended church with Gary. I attended Mass each week with him, even though I did not understand much about the Catholic faith.

When Gary received his degree, we moved to Brainerd, Minnesota, and he obtained his first job as an accountant with the firm of Freeman and Kummet Accounting. Brainerd is a tourist community of about 20,000 people. The city is surrounded by lakes and woods and is the mythical home of Paul Bunyan. We were content to make our home in Brainerd forever. We joined Saint Andrews Catholic Church and before long, I was involved in church events and had become a self-taught Catholic. After Tammy was born, we made the decision that I would be a stay-at-home mom. Volunteering as a teacher, I began with preschool and taught different age levels throughout the years. As I taught the classes, I learned as much or more from the students than I taught them. It amazes me that with my background I was not questioned about my faith or what qualifications I had to teach religion. I was on the Board for the Council of Catholic Women, even serving a term as president, and am currently a member of St. Anthony's Guild. Both Gary and I served on the church council.

For the most part, I focused on raising our three children, Tammy, Jeff, and Jennifer, involving myself in whatever they were doing. All three were active in sports, school, and church events. I learned to juggle schedules and keep the family on track. It was not unusual to see the Bluth family cheering each other on at any of the children's activities, be it basketball, baseball, volleyball, or band.

Family togetherness was what we treasured the most. We took advantage of the area we lived in and what it offered to the tourists. On our first vacation together, we rented a cabin 10 miles down the road at a resort in the Brainerd area. It was not unusual for us to take a babysitter along on vacation so that Mom and Dad could have a true vacation.

We went on other vacations, including driving to the Black Hills of South Dakota, to Grand Marais in Minnesota, and to Arizona. Planning a vacation was as much fun as the actual trip. And when we went through Gooseberry Falls, in the northern part of Minnesota, three of us would stand side by side and take pictures; we have numerous photos of the exact same scenery.

Tammy and I learned to ski and spent many weekends skiing the slopes of Spirit Mountain in Duluth, Minnesota. One particular weekend at Spirit Mountain, Gary and Jennifer went cross-country skiing for the first time while Tammy, Jeff, and I skied downhill. Gary and Jennifer took a wrong turn and began to realize they were no longer on the beginner paths but an advanced trail. They were not prepared to ski these challenging hills. In time, they realized the only safe way to return was to remove their skis and walk back to the chalet. We still laugh about their walking the slopes of Duluth rather than skiing them. After that, my husband put his skis up in the garage rafters where they still remain to this day, never to be used again.

After the children were all in school, I decided to go back to college for a master's degree in counseling. Saint Cloud State University offered an evening program in community counseling, and I was soon attending a class one night a week. This was a long-term goal, and I had a seven-year plan because I did not want to disrupt the family. I had done such a good job of taking care of my husband and children, they told me they were afraid they wouldn't be able to get along without me. I reassured them they were very capable and could easily manage that one night a week on their own.

We purchased some land on Gull Lake in the Brainerd area in the early 70s, and 10 years later, we built a small cabin that became our weekend getaway. Twenty years later, we live in that house we built. In the beginning, the brush on the lot was so thick we had to cut a path before we could see the other side. This problem created dozens of trips to the lake and back before we could begin to play there, but rather than dreading it, our family looked forward to clearing it. The reason was that our next door neighbors, Fred and Mary, had three children and a lot that also needed to be cleared. Their children Paul, Kari, and Jill were the same ages as our three children. So on weekends during the spring and summer, both families would be at the lake clearing brush, having bonfires, and roasting hot dogs.

We looked forward to spending time there as a family, sun-tanning, boating, and visiting with the neighbors. Tammy and I spent a lot of hours water-skiing around the island on Gull Lake; Gary spent hours pulling the children on water skis or playing baseball in the water.

Our lake property includes a big hill where the children could go sledding. I held my breath many times, thinking one of them would slam into the big oak tree at the bottom of the hill. With God's protection, none of them did. Our home was always open to other children. We served cup after cup of hot chocolate after a day of sledding or other winter activity. It was a way to warm our souls as well as our shivering bodies.

When my husband and I encountered some problems in our marriage, I talked to our priest about it. He referred me to a Christian counselor named Gene. During the time I counseled with him, he taught me how to pray, the importance of reading Scripture, and how to turn to Jesus as a friend. He also taught me the importance of the Eucharist and advised me to receive the Eucharist as often as possible. Learning about Jesus as a friend helped save our marriage. I prayed daily, turned to God for my needs, and began to use Him as a sounding board as well as a friend.

Growing up in an unassuming, modest family has taught me that many families started just like mine. My path in daily lessons has taken many turns that have made me who I am today. Going through the ups and downs and curves I experienced along my path of life has been the foundation for responsibility, reliability, creativity, and family togetherness, which has been the glue holding my family together during a crisis.

I am so thankful that we took time for family togetherness. Memories are precious and cannot be taken away when a tragedy occurs.

Chapter 3

No Blueprint

My family and I had to learn ways to deal with the tragedy of losing Tammy fairly quickly but lacked any blueprint for how to do that. Thank goodness for people who are not personally involved at the time of a tragedy. Terry and his compassionate wife, Cindy, shared with us the bad news yet stayed to comfort us as well. Terry and Cindy made decisions, offered information, and responded with details to our questions. They made decisions that, emotionally, I just couldn't do right then. I will forever be indebted to their kindness in bringing some calmness to a chaotic situation. Cindy made phone calls and invited friends to come and be with us. She called my sister, Lois, and Gary's partner at work, Lloyd. He and his wife, Rita, came over immediately and waited with us until our family members arrived. Those calls would have been too painful for me to make—any calls to tell others your child has died are far too painful to make. I wanted Lois to tell my mother in person. I did not want Grandma Charity to hear over the phone that her granddaughter had died.

I did not want Tammy's friends to have to hear about her death through the media. I had to let them know personally, so in the early hours of the morning, about 12:30, I called a friend of Tammy's named Mona and told her through my tears that Tammy had died in a car crash. She had many questions, but I had no answers. It was the hardest phone call I had ever had to make in my life. Mona was participating in a school volleyball tournament the next day. The players dedicated that game to Tammy's memory. It was a hard game for the friends, but one they had to play.

Tammy's friends' world had been shattered, as had mine. Seventeen-year-olds are not supposed to die. They are to be with you forever. Nothing is to interfere with their plans and dreams, especially not a tragic, unexpected death like the one that had just happened to Tammy. It wasn't fair.

News of Tammy's death spread like wildfire. Many people were affected by Tammy's death. Friends, family, acquaintances, and the entire community offered much support. Many came to our house and brought dinners, salads, cakes, pies, and cookies. At times we had standing room only in our kitchen, living room, and family room. My brother, Rocky, and sister, Lois, and their families and my mother arrived at our house around 2:30 a.m. on Saturday the 14th. It didn't matter that they arrived in the middle of the night. They had to be there for us and for themselves. We hugged each other and cried. My sister, Sharon, who lived in Arizona, arrived on a flight later on the 14th; and my brother Jim and his wife, Ruth, arrived on Sunday. My entire family was there to comfort us. The support, encouragement, and prayers were our lifelines for the next days, weeks, and months. I wouldn't have been able to survive the death of my child without the support from so many people. I would think it would be nearly impossible to do on your own.

People kept coming with sympathy and good wishes. Even when the support is so needed, receiving it can become overwhelming. Everyone had questions about what happened. We had to tell the story of how Tammy died over and over again, and the responses became both automatic and spontaneous. This was painful but also therapeutic. I had a tug of war going on in my heart: I wanted to talk about how Tammy died, but I didn't want to talk about it. I couldn't answer all the questions people had. I didn't have the answers. I wanted the support and comfort from friends and family, but I wanted some time alone too—to cry and to grieve. It was impossible to find the right balance for a long time.

Chapter 4

Difficult Decisions

We suddenly had to decide what kind of funeral to have for our 17-year-old daughter. We had been planning a graduation, and now, in the blink of an eye, we had to plan a funeral. Where do we start? The obvious place was to choose a funeral home. There are only two funeral homes in Brainerd, and since we were acquainted with personnel from both, the decision was tough. We chose the funeral home that we did because it could accommodate more people and had more parking. The second step was to make that dreaded call to begin coordinating funeral plans. As much as I didn't want to make these decisions, they had to be completed. There was no time to waste. These were not decisions that could wait for a day or a week or until we were ready to make them. We had to forge ahead.

Sitting down in the funeral home with the director was a horrible experience. Our emotions were so fragile. My brother, Rocky, went to the funeral home with Gary and me; we needed someone who could think straight and help us make decisions. I have no recollection of who else was with us. I don't even remember if Jeff and Jennifer were there. My memory of the whole process is foggy. I recall going into a room, which at the time seemed huge, filled with caskets. I thought, what do I look for in choosing a casket for my child? Do I want the inside lining to be pink, blue, white, or what? What kind of finish do we want on the outside of the casket? No one told us we would have to have a closed casket because of Tammy's condition, so we agonized over some of these decisions. I just wanted to scream, "I don't want to do this! I cannot pick out a casket! Please do not make me do this!" Somehow, we chose a casket. I imagine I had some input as to the final decision, but I don't remember. All that I recall is that the job was completed.

We next needed to decide in which cemetery to bury Tammy. We needed to take a drive out to the cemetery to choose a lot. Again, what do you look for in choosing a lot? We decided to look for a place where there would be room for five burial plots: one for Gary, Jeff, Jennifer, Tammy, and me. Then I thought Tammy would need a tree for some shade. That would be peaceful, I thought. The more decisions I had to make regarding the burial of my child, the more my thinking became confused. I didn't have the ability to contemplate everything that needed to be considered.

By the time we finished these arrangements, I was exhausted. I wanted to go home, sleep, and hope that I was only having a bad dream. I really wanted to go bury myself in a hole and come out when the funeral was over.

But that wasn't to be. The funeral plans were not completed, and time was of the essence. We had not planned the Mass for the funeral, nor did I know who would be pallbearers. What kind of flowers did we want? What songs should we sing? Who would do the readings? What time would the funeral be? How many should we plan for lunch after the funeral? I was so tired. My body ached everywhere, but there was no time for rest now. Rest would come later, much later. When this nightmare was over, maybe then I could rest. Not even 24 hours had gone by, yet I felt as if I had been planning the funeral for a week. Energy had drained out of me from my head to my toes. My body felt like a rag doll that no longer had any bone structure.

I began to ask God, "Where are You in all this? Why? Why now?" I called Gene, the clergyman who had counseled us earlier, to ask if he would help us. He came to our house and gave us advice on how to begin planning Tammy's funeral. A number of Tammy's friends were also invited to participate. Jeff, Jennifer, Gary, Gene, myself, and some of Tammy's friends sat around the dining room table to plan and reminisce.

It was marginally energizing being around them; hearing them talk about Tammy and what she meant to them was helpful. Having Tammy's friends participate in the arrangements was comforting for me and for them. There were more tears and even some laughter. It amazed me that I kept any sense of humor through even a bit of this tragedy. The laughter we shared was refreshing, though short-lived. Somehow, we managed to plan songs to be sung, readings to read, and people to participate in carrying them out. Mona, Jodi, Lisa, Steve, and Doug all read Scriptures or prayers during the Mass. These friends were great in offering support to us and especially to Jeff and Jennifer.

Darlene, a friend of the family, called and suggested we might want to put some of Tammy's meaningful possessions on display at the funeral home. For certain, God sent His angels to help me think when I could not do so on my own; I would not have thought of that. Lori, Darlene's daughter and a friend of Tammy's, came over and gathered photo albums, tennis shoes that Tammy wore for basketball games, the roses Tammy had received from Mike on Friday, and other mementoes that would remind people of her. These were displayed on a table at the funeral home. I wish I had had the foresight to take pictures of those things as displayed, since it would have been a comfort later.

Attending church on Sunday morning was our next hurdle. Going to St. Andrew's Church had been a part of our regular Sunday routine for the family since moving to Brainerd in 1968. I was torn inside. I wanted to go, but I didn't want to face all the people who'd be there. I didn't want anyone to feel sorry for me. I didn't want people to be uncomfortable seeing my pain.

I did, of course, go; it turned out to be a supportive experience. Many of my worries came true; others didn't. Some people apparently didn't know what to do and did nothing; some came and offered support; and others did not know the situation or us. We were hugged and given sympathetic words from many people. Tears flowed throughout the whole Mass. My husband held his arm around me to calm my trembling while I cried during the service.

No messages sank in while I sat there, but I knew through all this tragedy that God was still somewhere out there. I didn't know where, but I had developed a strong faith over the past years that I believed would sustain me.

Visitation was scheduled for Sunday afternoon, September 15th, beginning at 2:00 p.m., and a prayer service would begin at 7:30 p.m. Going to the funeral home the first time and then seeing the casket for the first time was a terrible experience; I collapsed in a chair and just sobbed. It had finally sunk in that we had to have a closed casket because Tammy's body had been burned beyond recognition. Knowing she was there—right there in the casket— and I couldn't see her was very painful. There was no way to acknowledge her presence and no way to say my final goodbye to her.

The room filled with flowers. It seemed as if the whole community sent flowers: red, yellow, and blue flowers as well as green plants. It was a beautiful, awesome sight; the sight and smell of the flowers was breathtaking. It was also overwhelming to know we had so much support and so many friends.

People began arriving at the funeral home when visitation began and continued to arrive for several hours afterward. I cannot remember what people said as they offered condolences, but I do remember that there were an amazing number of people who attended. I received many hugs from friends, family, and strangers. Teenagers came and offered support. Some of them did not want to leave. It was too much for them to handle. One of their peers was lying in the casket covered with a spray of roses. The teenagers kept touching the mementos that were there. It helped them to say goodbye to Tammy and brought some closure to her death.

Tears can be healing, and we shared them with everyone— some with people we knew well, some with people who were acquaintances, and some with complete strangers. I have learned not to worry about what to say to people when I go to a funeral home to offer condolences now, because though I don't remember what people said, I do remember who was there offering their support, and that is what matters in the end.

We began to hear speculation that the person who hit the car our daughter was in had been driving drunk. I didn't want to hear anything about that at that time—it was way too much to deal with just then. I wanted to get through this visitation and then the funeral. I wondered briefly how people could be repeating this awful rumor to us. It was inconceivable to think that perhaps a drunk driver had killed our daughter. *Stop, stop!* my mind screamed. *I can't take it!* The funeral was all I could get through right then. Just let me put the killer out of my mind for the next few days, and I will deal with that later.

I sent my prayers to God. *Please help me, God. It cannot be true that I have to bury my daughter. Her death could have been prevented.* It was later when anger started to set in, but I had no time or energy for anger then.

After visitation, I returned home and saw that more food, flowers, and people continued to arrive. *Was there no end? Was there no end to what people would do for us?* People wanted me to eat. I could not. Food had no appeal, but people keep offering. It made them feel as if they were doing something. I took a plate of food and set it down. Advice came from all sides—some good, some meaningless—but everyone meant well. Others were concerned about my not having enough strength to go on, so they insisted I eat. *Please leave me alone,* I thought. *I have been able to decide for myself for years when I will eat and when I won't. Do not take that away from me now. My life feels so out of control. Let me have that piece of control for myself.* I felt helpless. Other people felt helpless. There was nothing anyone could say or do that would bring Tammy back.

I was worn out by the time the last of the visitors left the house, but I couldn't sleep, and I couldn't relax. I would lie down but my eyes wouldn't shut. I was afraid that if I fell asleep, I might never wake up. I rested and dozed.

Tomorrow will be the funeral. How will that go? I wish I could skip that part. Can't I just run away and not go to the funeral? What is appropriate attire for a mother to wear to her daughter's funeral? Will anyone come? How do I act? What if Tammy's friends don't show up to do the readings? The questions that kept coming often didn't make sense, but they consumed my thoughts. I wondered how Jeff and Jennifer would get through the funeral. *What was going through their minds? How do they feel about what they'd been through so far?*

What Jeff and Jennifer had had to endure in the past two days was more than teenagers should have had to experience. It wasn't fair to them. It wasn't their fault. *Were they blaming themselves? What had others said to them? How have their friends comforted them?*

I was supposed to be trying to sleep, but the storm of questions wouldn't cease. I dreaded thinking about the next day. Burying my daughter would put an end to our 17 years together. I was afraid to think of what that meant to me, and I didn't want to deal with it. *How can I possibly get through a funeral for my daughter? It is not possible. There is no way I can do this. Can't somebody stop all these questions, these thoughts?* I wanted to shut my mind down, but the thoughts whirled through the night. *How will the other children be able to go back to school? They will not be able to function. I will never leave this house again. I will not be able to function ever again.* The thoughts just keep coming. I cannot remember them all. I began to think I was going crazy. *I will feel like this the rest of my life.*

There is no way I will ever find any happiness again. Tears consumed me. I cried myself to sleep. It was difficult not to be able to comfort my husband and kids, but I had none to give. I felt that my ability to be a mother to Jeff and Jennifer has been taken away. I was filled with my own hurt and pain. It was impossible to think about caring for anyone else now. I just needed to survive the night. I called out, "God, are you there?" Sleep finally took over, and I shut down for a few hours. I woke up again, though, and the same questions and more raced through my mind again. Tears, questions, sleep—the pattern continued for the rest of the night.

Chapter 5

Final Goodbye

When I woke from my shaky sleep in the morning, my mind was immediately overloaded: This is the day of Tammy's funeral. I was exhausted and wondered what I would do until three in the afternoon. *Why did we plan the funeral for so late in the day? Is it too late to change the time? Let's have the funeral first thing in the morning. Won't these questions and thoughts ever stop? Get yourself together,* I thought. *Your kids need you.* I began the day because I had to, not because I was ready to face it. The morning passed talking to relatives and friends.

We arrived early at the funeral home for our last chance to see the casket with Tammy in it. I wanted one last glimpse of my daughter before having to say the final goodbye. I wanted to hold her and tell her I loved her and find a way to say goodbye. I could only do that to the casket. It seems so cold and unreal to be talking to a wooden box surrounded with flowers. Some of the flowers have disappeared. They must have been taken to the church. I cannot believe how active my mind is. The thoughts just would not stop. I wanted a break. The next few hours would seem like an eternity.

I went back to saying goodbye to Tammy. There were no words that could comfort me in saying goodbye to my daughter. I couldn't hold her. I couldn't touch her. I couldn't stroke her hair. I began to think, *What if I forget what she looks like? What is in that casket? How much of Tammy's body is in the casket? What condition is it in?* I was certainly too afraid of the answer to that question to really want to know it at that point. *Maybe later I can find that answer.* I could express no words, only pour tears of goodbye. I loved my daughter, and I should not have had to go through that. I wanted to see her graduate. The minutes kept ticking away.

The time finally came for the family to leave the funeral home and go to the church. I will never forget how I felt when I walked into that church behind Tammy's friends and pallbearers—Paul, Jay, Tom, Mike F., Dan, and Jared. Taking a step inside the church and seeing all the people was shocking. I was stunned with the size of the crowd. I cannot ever remember that many people in our church. The love of the community overtook me. I had not been prepared for this outpouring of people and their love. It touched my heart very deeply. I could not restrain the tears. I didn't know if they were triggered because of having to bury my daughter or because I felt the overwhelming support of hundreds of people in our church. My husband had to help me down the aisle. The youth choir that Tammy had been a part of was singing a song. I looked up on the altar, and there were six priests all dressed in white. The sight of all the priests at the altar surprised me. I had never seen six priests at the altar before, and they were there to give a Mass for my daughter.

The funeral began. Tammy's friend, Mona, began it with the following reading:

"Welcome to all of you as we gather together in prayer and song to remember Tammy Marie Bluth and support her family and one another. This reflection is entitled 'A Time for Tears.'"

There is a time for tears, a time when people have no one to turn to, a time when they do all the right things and yet come to grief.

There is a time when life seems godforsaken and when we feel more acutely the dust of the earth than the breath of God.

There is a time when the heavens are dark and the disciples are gone, a time when a few nails and unbearable pain are the only remains of a kingdom.

There is a time when Easter seems absurd and resurrection impossible, a time when the tomb seems more credible than the Fatherhood of God.

There is a time when we are baffled and bewildered and when all we can say is "Father, into your hands…Father, into your hands."

There is a time when such a time comes. And Christians have no answers at such a time. All they can say is that even God knew a time for tears, and that in it He did not despair.

The choir sang "For Those Tears I Died," "Hosea," "Whom Should I Fear," and "You Are Near."

Steve read first from the book of Wisdom, 4:7-14. Doug did the second reading from the first letter of John, 3:1-2. Intermittently during the Mass, the choir sang "Be Not Afraid," "Prayer of St. Francis," "And I Will Follow," "Only a Shadow," "Before the Sun Burned Bright," "On Eagles Wings," and "Friends."

"Be Not Afraid" and "On Eagles Wings" began to take on new meaning to me. The songs that I had sung many times before began to speak very loudly to me. I was comforted, and for a moment, I thought I glimpsed God touching me.

If there ever was a time I wished I had a tape recorder, it was during the homily given by Father Mike. I know he said some beautiful words about Tammy, but I don't recall specifically what they were. My mind was too cluttered with too many thoughts about Tammy to take in what he said. Following the homily, the prayers of the faithful were read by Lisa and Janelle. The prayers were composed by Tammy's friends and reads as follows:

Father Mike: "We believe that Tammy now lives with Jesus, who is the resurrection and the life. Believing that Jesus is Lord, we turn to Him in prayer, that we might be willing to listen to the pain of others as Tammy did so often and so well; we pray to the Lord, [all] Lord hear our prayer.

"For the strength to imitate her sense of humor and attitude of hopefulness that she gave to others, we pray to the Lord, [all] Lord hear our prayer.

"For an attitude of readiness to help and share unconditionally as Tammy did, we pray to the Lord, [all] Lord, hear our prayer.

"That we might be as trustworthy as she was, we pray to the Lord, [all] Lord, hear our prayer.

"That we might be able to be as honest as possible without breaking a confidence, we pray to the Lord, [all] Lord, hear our prayer.

"For the ability to laugh and bring others out of depression as Tammy did, we pray to the Lord, [all] Lord, hear our prayer."

Father Mike concluded with "God our Father, we trust You to put our troubled hearts at rest. We ask for Your comfort and strength through Jesus our Lord and friend. Amen."

The tears dripped down my face. I could get through this service; relief that my daughter's funeral was coming to an end was reassuring. One last prayer, one last song, and the church service would be over. My body started to calm down. The combination of tears, comfort, and calm caused a jumble of emotions inside.

Final Goodbye

At the conclusion of the Mass, Jodi read the following:
"And what does it mean to mourn?"
Tammy asked the multitude.
And she stepped forward and said:

To mourn is to be given a second heart.
It is to care so deeply
That you show your ache in person.

To mourn is to be unashamed of tears.
It is to be healed
And broken
And built up
All in the same moment.

Blessed are you if you can minister to others
With a heart that feels
With a heart that hurts
With a heart that loves
And blessed are you if you can minister to others
With a heart that serves
And a heart that sees the need before it's spoken.
To mourn is to forget yourself for a moment
And get lost in someone else's pain
And then,
To find yourself
In the very act of getting lost.
To mourn is to be an expert
In the miracle
Of being careful with another's pain.

It is to be full of the willingness
Of forever reaching out to
And picking up

And holding carefully
Those who hurt.
To mourn is to sing with the dying
And to be healed
By the song
And the death.

"God has loved us and touched our lives in our experiencing the gift of the many different ways Tammy's life showed that she loved, that she cared, that she understood, that she forgave, that she would try again. Each of you is invited to reflect on a way that you experienced Tammy's goodness, and in your heart say, 'Thank you, Lord.'"

Walking out of church behind the casket is something that I, as a mother, will never forget. It is not anything that I would wish on anyone. It was difficult to conceive that the time had come to place my daughter in her final resting place. A myriad of emotions were released when I turned down the aisle with weakened knees and saw all the people grieving with me and my family. On the one hand, I appreciated all their support that brought comfort; but on the other hand, it was difficult to look at the pain on their faces. That short walk out of the church was probably the longest walk I have ever taken. My whole body felt numb with pain and exhausted from lack of sleep. Soon would be the final ending to a long, distressing, exhausting three days.

Everyone in the car was silent on the way to the cemetery, perhaps thinking of their individual last moments with Tammy. We kept the thoughts quiet in each of our hearts, those final thoughts too precious and personal to speak out loud. Arriving at the cemetery and seeing the big mound of dirt and the dark, cold hole to put my daughter in was too much. I lost control of my emotions. The pain began in my toes and slowly worked its way up and out of my body. More tears. I sobbed. *How can I let this go on?* I think. *I have to. I can get through this. Just let me sit in the car. I cannot bear to see the casket placed over the top of that deep, dark hole. I must; there is no other choice.* The thoughts keep coming at a ferocious pace. *What if I do not go see this? I am strong enough to do this. What are my kids thinking? I feel helpless, knowing there is no time to process feelings. The people are beginning to gather around the casket.* Somehow, I managed to leave the car and walk up to the front row right next to the casket. Even though the service at the cemetery only takes minutes, it seemed to take years off my life. I leaned over the casket, gave my daughter one final kiss, said, "I love you," and turned to leave. I could not stay one more second. I turned my back on the casket and went to the car. I did not look back. That was the final goodbye.

I was quiet and somber walking back to the car. There was some sense of relief that the funeral was over. A lightness began to come over me; realizing that my daughter was safe in the arms of God was comforting, though I would rather have had her safe in my arms. Knowing God was with her did not take the pain away, but it did bring me calm for the rest of the day.

On the surface, it appeared that the grief was over and behind us, but it had only really just begun.

Chapter 6

More Bad News

Apparently, one person's fun became our family's tragedy. A few days following the funeral, a Minnesota State Patrol Officer in full official uniform came to our door and wanted to talk to us regarding Tammy's car wreck. Seeing the patrol officer at our door was unexpectedly frightening and intimidating. *What would he have to say to us? What questions would I have to ask him? What questions did I want answers to at this point?* He confirmed for us that the person responsible for Tammy's death had been driving drunk. He'd had a blood alcohol content of 0.17 percent; blood alcohol content needs to be 0.10 to be legally intoxicated while driving in Minnesota. We had heard rumors, but until the State Patrol Officer confirmed it, they remained just that. The officer was matter-of-fact when he gave us the news, but was probably uncomfortable having to give us more bad news.

While I'd heard about the drunk driver, I could not at that time think about anything else or anyone else. All I could handle was my own pain inside. Now I had to deal with the fact that someone being irresponsible, criminal even, had killed my daughter.

I didn't want to hear that there was a drunk driver involved; it would add too much to the grieving process. My immediate reaction was anger. I began to seethe with rage, thinking, *How dare this person drink, drive, and then kill my daughter?!* Then abruptly my anger turned to numbness and I just went limp. *What else would I have to go through because of what this man did?* The information we received that day was fairly sketchy. Perhaps it was because of the pain I was going through that I couldn't think clearly, so that the questions I had didn't surface. Perhaps it was because I did not want to hear any more bad news—if I didn't ask the questions, then I wouldn't have to know any more painful details.

I'd always assumed that drunk drivers were only a problem after the bars closed at 1:00 in the morning. I hadn't realized it was possible that drunk drivers could be on the highway at other times of the day. In fact, I was very naive in my knowledge about drunk driving. My daughter was killed about 10:00 in the evening, so my assumption did not hold true anymore.

The Patrol Officer was not at our house very long and left stating that if we had any questions we should be sure to call him.

October 19th, just a few weeks after Tammy's death, would have been Tammy's 18th birthday. We had talked many times about what it would be like to be 18. She could hardly wait to become an adult and begin making her own decisions. She often said that once she was 18, she would no longer have to obey Mom and Dad's rules. Now she wouldn't have the opportunity to become an adult and test her own ability to develop rules of her own. As a mother, I wanted my children to be able to experience all of life and to try out things for themselves. I was so angry that Tammy could not live her life to the fullest.

Many questions kept haunting me as Tammy's birthday approached. *How do you celebrate the birthday of your daughter who is dead? Would it be appropriate for me to bake a cake? What would I do to get through this birthday that Tammy so looked forward to celebrating?* After much agonizing, I decided to celebrate, have a cake, and invite friends over to celebrate it with us. The idea was good, and the friends were willing to come. After the friends arrived at our house, however, the question became, *What should we do next?* It was rather uncomfortable for all of us. No one talked about Tammy. I waited for the others to bring up her name, and the others waited for me to begin talking about her. None of us took the risk.

Chapter 7

Nightmare in Court

Since Tammy was killed by a drunk driver, that meant a court hearing would take place. I had no previous experience with the criminal justice system, so I didn't know what to expect. In the past, I had watched some Perry Mason programs on television that showed some courtroom drama. The "bad guy" always lost and had to pay the consequence for his behavior, which pretty much informed my whole knowledge about court proceedings, which represents the State of Minnesota's interest versus the offender's, which I also didn't know at the time. It was not the Bluth's against Richard, the offender. It was the State of Minnesota against Richard. Since a drunk driver killed our daughter, our family had now earned the label of "victim." We were a drunk-driving statistic at the local, state, and national level.

Gary had heard from our civil attorney as to when the offender would be going to court. I wanted to be in the courtroom to see this man severely punished for taking our daughter so tragically from us. I expected a jury trial like the ones I'd seen so many times on television. Gary had had one short conversation with the prosecuting attorney, Steve; he didn't tell us what to expect in the court proceedings, and he gave us limited information regarding the charges against the person who killed Tammy. On Monday,

December 2, 1985, the morning of the court hearing at the court-house in Brainerd, 60 days after Tammy's death, we met our civil attorney in the parking lot as he was walking away from the court-house. Passing by us, he greeted us and said he was on his way to a meeting. I was dumbfounded. Up to that time, I'd thought he'd be involved with the case. *If our case was scheduled for that morning, why was he heading in another direction for another meeting?*

My husband and I went into the courthouse. Minnesota v Richard would be held in the courtroom on the third floor. We walked up the three flights, and by the time we got there, I was completely out of breath and needed some time to get it back. The courthouse felt cold and detached; I felt no warm, fuzzy feelings about justice and truth coming from that building. Anxiety increased steadily inside me. I was scared and very apprehensive about what to expect. I knew I didn't want to miss out on whatever was about to happen, but just being in the courthouse was intimidating. And I kept wondering if our attorney would get back in time for the beginning of the court proceedings. It simply didn't occur to me that he would never be involved in the case.

Opening the courtroom door and walking inside was traumatic. Peering inside the courtroom for the first time was even worse. The first thing I saw when opening the courtroom door was a room full of people. My first thought was, *Who are all these people and why are they here?* I knew I was in the right place, but did not understand what was happening. After opening the door, taking that first step in, and seeing all the people, I was emotionally blasted. We had to find a place to sit. My mind whirled with questions but had no one to answer them. Looking up to the front of the room and seeing the judge's chair elevated and empty gave me a cold feeling all over. Off to the left side of the courtroom were 12 empty captain's chairs I assumed were for the jury. Then I thought that maybe all these people in the courtroom were perspective jurors.

I hated being so unprepared.

As the judge came into the courtroom, everyone had to stand. I thought he would explain the procedure and what to expect. No such luck. When the other peoples' names were called, I soon realized that the other people in the courtroom were for other cases scheduled at the same time as ours. We were just a number on the court docket for the State of Minnesota versus the defendant. Neither our names nor Tammy's was ever mentioned, and it could have been any case, not the one for the murder of our daughter. I certainly didn't feel that anyone in the courtroom had a concern about our family, even though we had lost our daughter, Tammy.

When our case number was called, the judge went on to state this was a "continued" first appearance, although the defendant had already had a pre-plea pre-sentencing investigation. I had no idea what this meant or its significance. The defense attorney, Max, stated it was the intention of the defendant, Richard, to enter a plea of guilty to the charge and proceed to sentencing today.

The judge asked the defendant some questions about whether he understood what was happening and if he had any concerns. *Wait a minute,* I thought. *No one was asking us any questions about what we understood, or if we had any concerns.* If my anger hadn't been on the front burner before, it certainly was now, listening to what was taking place. I was livid.

The defendant, Richard was charged with "criminal vehicular operation of a motor vehicle resulting in death." The judge asked the defendant how he pled to the charge and the defendant said, "Guilty." I thought, *You bet you're guilty, and I can't wait to see the tough sentence you're going to get for killing Tammy. You are the person responsible for taking our daughter from us. We will never see her again, but you still have your life.*

Richard had to swear an oath, and he was told he'd be asked some questions about his knowledge of his rights as a person accused of a crime. It was also explained to the defendant that if he didn't understand any of the questions he could say so. If at any time the defendant wanted to consult with his attorney, all he had to do was let the court know. He was then asked some questions, "What is your full name? Do you have a Minnesota driver's license? Did you own your vehicle? What education and training have you had? Can you read and write the English language?" I was thinking, *What does this have to do with Tammy's death?* I was completely uncomfortable with what was happening in that courtroom.

The questions continued. "Did you receive from your attorney at the time he first started to represent you a statement of rights as a person accused of a crime? Did you read that statement of rights? Did you understand it? Do you have any questions for the Court about your rights?" About now, I was furious. Inside my little voice was demanding I ask, *What about my rights? What are they? Doesn't anyone care? Do you know that Tammy's family is in the courtroom too?*

The judge continued to get clarification from the defendant that he understood everything concerning his rights and that he understood what was happening if he pleaded guilty that day. The judge was very precise about the defendant's understanding and knowing his rights.

Steve, prosecuting attorney, asked Richard, "Why don't you tell the Court in your own words how this collision occurred?"

Richard answered, "I really can't remember quite what happened. I was on my way home after work, and I struck the car on Highway 210 East in front of the restaurant, Hasse's Drop Inn."

(Steve) "Had you been drinking?"

(Richard) "Yes."

(Steve) "Where had you been drinking?"

(Richard) "Vilo Lanes and Pauline's."

(Steve) "What time did you start and what time did you stop? The collision occurred at ten twenty-one p.m."

(Richard) "I started shortly before five o'clock, and shortly before the accident I quit."

(Steve) "What were you drinking?"

(Richard) "Tap beer."

(Steve) "How many beers would you estimate that you had at Vilo's?"

(Richard) "A pitcher, probably."

(Steve) "How many beers would you say you had at Pauline's?"

(Richard) "Two to three."

(Steve) "Those are the two places that you went to first?"

(Richard) "We also went to Jeff's Bar and had some beer."

(Steve) "How many beers would you say you had at Jeff's Bar?"

(Richard) "Three."

(Steve) "Do you agree that you were driving while under the influence of alcohol?"

(Richard) "Yes."

(Steve) "You know that because you had a blood test taken which showed an alcohol level of point-one-seven percent, is that correct?"

(Richard) "Yes."

(Steve) "And as a result of the accident, Tammy Bluth, a passenger in the car you struck, was killed, is that correct?"

(Richard) "Yes."

There were no further questions at that point.

Now the case was ready to be sentenced. The next statements by the prosecuting attorney shocked me. Steve said, "I believe that the parents of the victim are in the courtroom. I believe they are represented by counsel, and they may want to provide some input." I'm thinking, *Represented by counsel? Now who would that be? I saw our attorney outside going someplace else.* I was unprepared and surprised for this. I stood up and said, "I would like to see him punished for drunk driving and not have the drinking excused because I think something has to be done about driving while drunk." I was intimidated about the whole procedure and certainly wasn't prepared to say anything.

What happened next brought me right out of my seat. Max, the defense attorney, had a character witness speak for the defendant.

"Your Honor, I am a fellow worker and employer of the defendant at the present time. I guess I have known him for eight years since I moved to Brainerd. I plea for leniency in his sentencing, knowing the individual, the person very well. He is a very stable, very good co-worker and employee. This is something which is an accident. I am sure that seventy-five percent of us in the courtroom could have possibly had the same circumstances happen to us. After we are through with this present job in St. Cloud, being in construction work and doing bigger jobs, we normally travel quite extensively all over the country. A long jail sentence, I believe, would be a problem, which is certainly not going to help matters with this suffering because he is personally suffering, quite extensively right now. That is all, Your Honor."

The tears rolled down my cheeks. I couldn't believe this was happening. They were asking for a lenient sentence because his job would be inconvenienced. I was screaming inside. The anger began to consume me. I wasn't sure I could sit through any more of this. *Did you forget the reason we are in this court process is because my daughter was killed? Did you ever feel any sense of concern for us?*

The defendant's wife, Cindy, had written a letter that was read in court by the defense attorney.

The letter reads as follows:

To whom it may concern:
Not a day has passed that Dick and I have thought about how this tragedy affected so many people, people we know and have a strong bond with and our families that we love very much.

Dick and I have two beautiful children. Our daughter is four years old, and our son just turned one. We look at this and think how it must feel to lose a child. We will have to live the rest of our lives with the realization that because of a terrible mistake, a child is gone from the people who loved and cared for her.

This weighs heavily on our thoughts, in our hearts. It is very difficult to live with. It is something that in order to deal with you must have to have a strong faith in God, and do it together as a family.

Dick and I ask that our children not be made to suffer because of this mistake. Too many people have suffered already. Dick is a wonderful father, very close to his children.

When I think of Dick and his two children being separated, I feel it would be another real tragedy.

I truly believe that for children to grow up with a strong value system they need the presence and love of both parents. Our daughter is at a very vulnerable age. Her daddy means the world to her. Our son is changing and learning new things every day.

Dick is a good, honest person and projects strong positive morals to his children. I know and anyone else that knows Dick realizes that this terrible car accident was an isolated incident in his life. He values life and would never intentionally injure another human being.

Dick and I believe in law and justice, but isn't there some way this can be accomplished without any more innocent people suffering? Children mean the world to us.

We ask that Dick be able to be home with his family and be able

to be a father to his children. Please consider the effect it would
have on our children if their father was not able to be there for
them.
    —*Cindy*

I was fit to be tied. Our daughter, Tammy, was dead, and now I had to sit in the courtroom and hear about how hard it would be for this man to be away from his children. *Had anybody considered how hard it would be for us to be away from our daughter the rest of our lives? How come the defendant's side was prepared? Didn't we have any rights?* The questions inside me were screaming to be heard. *Where was an apology? Doesn't your family care that our daughter was killed and that we will never see her again?* We will not be able to parent her again or to see her grow up. I wanted to scream, "Hey, remember us? We are a real live family with real feelings, and this is too much. Don't forget what happened to us. Don't just think about yourselves."

The final blow to me was when the defense attorney stood up and said the following words to make his case to the judge, "We have in this case some competing circumstances. Society has passed a law, the Minnesota legislature has passed a law, that makes criminal vehicular operation a crime in this particular instance, and negligence combined with a blood alcohol level of over point ten percent means a conviction for a felony. Society needs punishment for that, and the legislature has spoken strongly in the area of drunk driving. I am very well aware of that, and I believe I am very well aware of the Court's attitude toward that.

"We have another factor here, and that is a family has lost a daughter, a very lovely daughter, from all indications that I have been able to see from the newspaper articles and contacts I know from being a member of this community. That is very sad.

"There are two considerations here. There is another consideration, and that is the defendant and his family situation because it will not be just him that will suffer as a result of this. Richard knows that he has to pay the price for what happened. I have discussed that with him. He has acknowledged it. He is not trying to duck his responsibility. He is not trying to hide and say no, that he didn't do it. He was just careless. He is not trying to say that but for the grace of God, blame it on someone else, or it could have been the next Joe Blow coming down the road that could have done the same thing. He is not doing that. I think that is an indication that we are not dealing with the type of a sentence that should go up to a year. Of course, Richard is aware that the Court can impose probationary jail time of up to one year as a condition of probation for this particular kind of offense.

"I really think, Your Honor, though, substantially less jail time in this instance is indicated. The last time I appeared before this Court and represented someone charged with this particular offense, I think that the circumstances were much more egregious than they are here today. First of all, in that case, there were two people that were killed. The negligence, I think, was a good deal more serious, and I think also that the person involved wasn't too much younger than Richard but was a completely different type of individual.

"I think that this is clearly an aberration for him. In the case of the other person that I represented, to be very honest, I think I would have to say that is not the type of thing that he did regularly. In other words, getting intoxicated to excess and then endangering his life and that of innocent others on the highway afterwards. I don't think that is Richard you see standing before you. He is a solid member of this community. He has a family that he has got to be responsible for, a wife and two small children. It would not be productive for him to be incarcerated for such a long period of time. He might very well lose his job out of it, which would then place an additional burden on the people of this county.

"The court has remarked to me on occasion that there is a

right sentence for everybody, and I believe that. I think that is very true. In this instance, I think that a jail sentence in the area of ninety days would be an appropriate punishment for the offense. Perhaps the Court might consider some community service work in some particular field that would be beneficial to this community, lecturing of some kind. I guess I am kind of groping for suggestions along those lines. I think the type of punishment of up to a year in jail is not indicated in this case, and I don't think it would be the right sentence for the defendant."

Steve, the prosecuting attorney, stood up and made his case to the judge. He recommended that the defendant be sentenced to an eighteen-month prison sentence, execution of that sentence be stayed, and Richard be placed on probation for a period of five years on conditions set out by the Court.

"We would recommend that those conditions include one year in the county jail on a work release, a fine or community service in lieu of the fine, and refrain from consuming alcohol. The reason for this recommendation is that I am sure that the defendant feels regrets for what occurred. Anyone would, but the legislature has provided that when someone drives while intoxicated and causes the death of another person, it is a serious offense.

"I don't think ninety days in the county jail would be appropriate response to the offense committed. I would point out to the Court that the victim in this case in no way contributed to her death. That fact separates this from other cases in which, for example, two people are out drinking together; and it is a one-car accident, and the passenger is killed. This is not a case like that. This victim did not contribute to the accident.

"Also, I think that a sentence of ninety days as a condition of probation would be giving the wrong significance to the community. I don't believe this happens to seventy-five percent of the people. I don't believe seventy-five percent of the people would be driving with a blood alcohol of point-one-seven percent, but unfortunately, a substantial percentage does from time to time. I think that the Court has an opportunity in this case to send a message to the community. If one drives with that kind of blood alcohol and causes the death of another person, that the penalty they will have to pay will be substantial. The way to cut down the percentage of people who voluntarily over an extended period of time drink to excess on a Friday night and then drive home is to make it real clear that kind of conduct is not going to go unpunished, particularly if it results in a serious injury.

"We give a ninety-day jail sentence to people who are picked up and don't hurt anybody, but are simply driving intoxicated and have a prior record. This defendant doesn't have a prior record. The consequences of this behavior and, to a certain extent, it was voluntary behavior, were tremendous. I think the defendant should have to pay the maximum penalty permitted under the guidelines, not only because of the offense he committed, but also for its effect on the community."

After the defense attorney gave his summary and again asked a ninety-day sentence, I could feel myself rising out of my seat. Steam seemed to be coming out of my ears and mouth, I was so angry. I gasped very loudly in the courtroom, as I could not believe what was taking place. When the prosecuting attorney gave his remarks, I cannot remember hearing much of what he had to say as I was trying to sort out in my mind what I'd just heard. My daughter was dead, and this defense attorney wanted the person responsible to serve a ninety-day sentence because of how his family had already suffered. I wanted to scream so loudly that the whole community could hear my response.

John, an attorney we knew, was in the courtroom on another case and came over and asked me if I wanted to say something. You bet I wanted to say something, but what?

I stood up and uttered these words, "The defendant has never contacted us and never said he was sorry. I mean, if he is a good individual and a good upstanding community member, I am wondering where he has been the last 60 days. I also agree with the prosecuting attorney that the community cannot allow people to drink and drive and kill somebody and get 90 days for that. I think that is just terrible if that happens.

"I would also like to see the maximum sentence that he can receive be given. Our daughter will not ever return to us. He can be a father again in 18 months. We will never have our daughter back, and justice has to be done. We feel a lot of pain. We will suffer the rest of our lives. We cannot allow people to drink to 0.17 percent alcohol content and drive home and be allowed to do that."

After I spoke in the courtroom, the defendant's wife asked to be heard. These are her words, "I would like to comment and explain why I didn't contact you. When something like this happens, you don't know what to do. I can truthfully say Dick and I wanted to contact you so many times, but it couldn't make things better for you. How do you know what to do in a situation like this? We can look at our daughter and think if it happened to her, how we would feel. I didn't think you would want us to contact you right now, but in the future, I would like to be able to talk to you, and I would like you to know that I truly don't believe talking to you would have benefited you at all.

"I know that something has to be done, but I don't see how making our kids suffer can make it right again. I know something has to be done, and I would like people to realize what it can do to the family if they are the people that hurt somebody; and I think I will make it a goal of my life to help people realize what it can do to both of the families. I agree too that something has to be done, and I make a promise that I will try to help people understand what it does to both sides of the family."

Because these words were not from the defendant himself, they really had no meaning to me. I needed to hear from the person responsible for killing my daughter, not from his wife. (To my knowledge, nothing has been done to make good on that promise made on that December day in 1985.)

The defense attorney now tried to make sense of what just happened in the courtroom between the defendant's wife and me. He states, "Your Honor is very well aware of what has taken place in the last 10 or 15 minutes here in the courtroom as being a real conflict between the various values, and we have the Victim's Rights Act, and we have society's need for punishment. Yet, we have an individual who is appearing before the court for sentencing at this time who is deserving of justice as well as fair treatment based upon his particular circumstances and conditions.

"I really don't think what the other people have said makes any difference. The court, by pronouncing sentences in every case, is not necessarily going to send a message to the community in every case. That is a side benefit at times to the sentencing procedure. What is important, however, is not what the public thinks of this sentence but how the defendant is treated. Is the system treating him fairly? I think that is the largest consideration that the court has to consider here. He is not getting away scot-free without any punishment. Nobody is suggesting that. He doesn't suggest it, I don't suggest it, and his wife doesn't suggest it. I think that in this instance, what I said before still stands."

The judge then addressed the defendant, asking him if he had anything to say. The defendant said the following, "Yes. I have two children of my own, and I couldn't imagine losing one of them from an accident of this type. Like my wife said, I would have contacted the family, but I just didn't know what to say. I didn't know just what to do. I know there has got to be laws and justice. I know I have got to pay the price for what I have done, but I just wish that my children wouldn't have to suffer anymore either. That's it."

As the defendant was asked if he had anything to say, I thought that he perhaps would have taken that opportunity to give our family an apology. What was evident to me at that time was he was only concerned about his family and himself. I could see no evidence of his taking responsibility for Tammy's death. He had a perfect opportunity to look at Gary and me and say something, but he chose not to do so.

Chapter 8

The So-Called Sentence

All that remained was for the judge to pronounce his sentence. "It is ordered that an imposition of sentence be stayed for a period of five years from today unless prior to the expiration of said sentence has been revoked or you have been discharged. It is further ordered that you are herewith placed and will be upon probation during the continuance of said stay under the supervision of the Commissioner of Corrections upon the following terms and conditions:

"First, that you be confined to the County Jail, County of Crow Wing, State of Minnesota, for a period of one year to give you an opportunity to reflect upon your past actions, reconsider your present moral obligations to the community, and be prepared to live within the laws, rules, orders, and dictates of society. It is provided, however, that you be given the benefits of MSA 631.425 for work release pursuant to the Huber Law under the sole discretion of the sheriff's office to determine what your work hours are, what hours of the day you are to be released for such work, and the amount you are required to pay the county for your maintenance in and out of jail. The sheriff's department is authorized to revoke this Huber privilege without notice and in their sole discretion.

"That you devise a program of community service in the sum

of 500 hours under the auspices of the Probation Department, and once that program is devised and accepted by the department, you are to keep that up and fulfill that community service requirement. I would suggest that you have a valuable experience to share with the members of the community. You go to church organizations or to support groups and others and give your message as to what happens to your side of the family. I would suggest that you check the victim's side of the family, also, and you can have a valuable experience to share.

"That you hereinafter be of good behavior. You be a law-abiding citizen. You do not violate any laws or ordinances of any political subdivision.

"That you hereinafter and while on probation, obey and comply in all respects with all rules, regulations, standards, and orders promulgated for your conduct by the adult corrections people. You are to report immediately to the probation officer, and from time to time in the future when he requires your presence.

"That you hereinafter refrain from the use and consumption of any and all intoxicants. No beer, no liquor, no wine, no chemicals, no drugs, no dope, no anything that gives you a 'high' condition. In conjunction therewith, you are to submit to chemical testing upon the request of any probation officer or certified peace officer, which is on a spot-check basis without the necessity of probable cause or any other reasonable grounds. They just merely ask you and you have to comply.

"Failure to pass the test by having any prohibited chemicals in your system will be a violation of your terms and conditions of probation. Failure to take the test will be a violation of your terms and conditions of probation.

"In conjunction herewith you are to be analyzed for the necessary alcohol support group that is necessary for your condition in life. If you are required to go through long-term chemical dependency treatment, you are to do whatever the probation department determines after they have you analyzed for an alcohol assessment.

"That you reimburse the County for disbursements of prosecution in these proceedings by paying the sum of three hundred fifty dollars to the Clerk of this Court, said sum to be paid on a payment schedule to be worked out with you by the probation department, and once that schedule is worked out you are to keep it.

"Pursuant to the Minnesota Rules of Criminal Procedure, Rule 27.3 subdivision five, you are hereby notified that you have the right of appeal to the Minnesota Supreme Court and, further, if you are unable to pay the cost of the appeal you may apply to appeal at state expense. Because a stay of imposition is involved, there will be no surcharge levied. The maximum of forty dollars is herewith forgiven.

"This court does not believe that anyone should be permitted to drink and drive in any amount. The amount of 0.17 percent is prohibitive, scandalous; it is way too much for anybody to be drinking and driving.

"Insofar as I am able to give a message to the community, the message is simply that I do not tolerate drinking and driving and will sentence accordingly. My past sentences reflect this attitude, and when we have an opportunity to pass sentence upon people who are charged with aggravated driving while under the influence, the record will reflect that we have sent a message.

"We must also send a message to the casual drinkers, or so-called social drinkers, who don't think much of the law. It applies to them. Any person who drinks and drives is a danger and menace to society.

"That is the gist of the evil that is involved. You drank and you drove, and you will have to pay the price. Unfortunate as it is, your family also has to pay the price, but that is a necessary by-product of punishing you.

"Insofar as we grant that to the family, we do, but that doesn't prevent you to get off scot-free or lessen your culpability in any sense of the word.

"Let commitment be issued forthwith. Sergeant at Arms, will you see that he is transported to the County Jail? Proceedings are in recess."

After the court proceeding ended, John (our attorney friend), who left the courtroom with us, asked if we understood the defendant's sentence. I said no. He explained that the defendant had been given one year in the county jail with the Huber privilege, so he could be released for work each day; he wouldn't be in jail during his working hours. He'd gotten no fine except for having to pay court costs of three hundred fifty dollars. After being released from jail, Richard would be on probation for five years. He'd also have to have a chemical dependency evaluation and would have to follow what the evaluator decided. He would have to work off 500 hours of community service, and the probation department could decide what he was to do for the community service.

I thought the defendant had been required to do some speaking to organizations and churches but was later told that this was only a suggestion. He could do that if he chose, but it wasn't a requirement.

Once I understood the sentence, I was furious. I couldn't believe that this killer would only have to serve one year in jail and could go to his job every day. What kind of a punishment was that for someone who had killed my daughter? I felt so helpless and defeated. There was nothing I could do. The sentence had been given. It was now over.

My faith in the justice system had just been destroyed. My expectations of what the court system would do and what actually happened were miles apart. I thought a long-term jail sentence was almost automatic. I wouldn't have dreamt in a million years that when a person was sentenced to jail that they could actually be released to report to work. The process just baffled me. I was stunned after I understood the sentence. I felt as if the court had forgotten that my daughter had died. *Where was justice when a person seven-*

teen years old had been murdered by a person driving while drunk?

The anger welled up inside me. I was furious with the court system. I felt victimized by the whole court process. As a victim, I didn't know if I had any rights. If I did, I certainly felt I had not received them. Everything that transpired in the court that day seemed to be only for the benefit of the defendant and his family. I was so full of rage I just wanted to strike out and get revenge. *What could I do next? Take what was just given to me or try to fight it; and if so, how? What could be done, if anything?*

There was no peace after that day in court. No peace, but a lot of anger, rage, and turmoil inside. I really had naively expected that I would feel some sense of peace after the person responsible for killing my daughter was sent to jail. I expected that the offender would be punished severely for what he'd done and that the court process would go smoothly. Instead of peace, I felt nothing but the most burning, fiery-red rage.

I learned quickly that the criminal justice system is not a fair procedure for victims. The defendant, the one who commits the crime, has all the rights. In the courtroom setting, the victim is a number without a face.

I believe our family should have been given a chance to prepare a statement of how the loss affected our family before Richard was sentenced. I felt totally discounted because I did not have the opportunity to have any input after having time to think about what I would have wanted to say. Our family had just experienced a devastating loss and needed time in advance to prepare a statement, not just be put on the spot and asked to say something on the spur of the moment. It was so unjust that the defendant had the rights and was apprised of his rights. Had I a right to prepare what I now know to be called a victim-impact statement, I might not have felt so victimized and frustrated and angry. Our family was the innocent party, yet we had no rights, while the defendant was allowed to exercise all of his rights.

Sitting in the courtroom that day was a rude awakening to me. I became incredibly angry and bitter when I realized the defendant was able to exercise rights that I did not have as a victim. The ultimate frustration was that I had already suffered the loss of my daughter; I never realized I would be faced with more suffering because of the inadequacies of the justice system. No one should have to feel the powerlessness I felt in the courtroom.

I wanted the defendant to have to take full responsibility for what he did. I wanted him to get several years in prison and be forced away from his family and daily routines. I wanted him to be put away for life. I would never have my family whole again, so why should he be able to get back together with his family? What I really wanted to do was go slap his face and tell him what an awful person he was. Instead, I had to remain silent and listen to what he wanted.

I later found out that it is highly unusual for the defendant to plead and be sentenced on the same day. Usually there is a day in court when the defendant will plead guilty or not guilty. Then a pre-sentence investigation is assigned. A sentencing date will be set weeks or months after a plea has been made. This gives all the parties involved time to prepare for the sentencing. To this day, I do not understand the reasoning for allowing Richard to plead and be sentenced on the same day.

Chapter 9

One Step Forward, Two Steps Back

Following the court process, I was so blazing-red angry I could barely breathe. And now there were some tough choices for me to make: I could do something with my anger or run from it.

I did not take lightly becoming a victim by having my daughter killed and being victimized the second time by the courts. I tend to be more of a fighter than a "sit down and take it" kind of person. I decided that courtroom nightmare should not happen to anyone else who had become a drunk-driving victim. *What could I do to help others?* It was too late to make any changes in what happened to us in the courtroom, but I could make a difference for others.

I had heard about Mothers Against Drunk Driving (MADD) but knew very little about what they stood for or what they were all about. I thought that maybe they could give me some guidance as to what to do for others. I immediately began to pursue finding out how to get a MADD chapter started in Brainerd. I wrote a letter to the MADD's national office in California (which is now located in Texas) to ask what I needed to do to help other victims.

I thought the process would consist of filling out a few pages of information, and then I could get started working with victims. It didn't work that way. MADD sent me a packet of information that described all the steps it would take to get a chapter started in our community, which was just overwhelming. I set the packet aside. In response to my letter, though, the National Office of MADD contacted the MADD State Office in Minnesota. Dennis, President of the Minnesota State organization, called to inform me that a woman named Bonnie Alexander had also inquired about starting a MADD chapter. Dennis was sympathetic about the death of my daughter and encouraged me to start a chapter.

I gave Bonnie Alexander a call, and she told me she was also interested in starting a chapter of MADD. She and her husband had divorced, and he was on his way to pick up their children for visitation when he, driving drunk, rolled his car and died in the one-car crash. She was angry because her children could have been in the car if he had picked them up first and then crashed.

Bonnie and I became acquainted and agreed that by working together we could handle MADD's requirements. The first thing we needed to do was find out what happened, legally, in our county regarding drunk driving. We needed to interview the judges, prosecuting attorneys, probation officers, law enforcement, and others who had anything to do with drinking and driving cases. We needed to gather statistics that showed the extent of the drunk driving in our area, and then we needed to fill out pages of information based on the facts and statistics we learned. We needed to have 20 paid members. We also needed to be aware of the attitude of our community and justice system regarding drinking and driving.

Bonnie and I decided to do the interviews together at the beginning. Just dialing the phone to set up appointments with the various people involved in the court process intimidated both of us. I had a notion in my mind that the people involved in the courts were very powerful and wouldn't want to bother with me, especially if I were to disagree with how they carried out the laws and statutes. I realized it might be a challenge to acquire any information from the people we were to talk with, as there would be considerable disagreement between what I thought and what they thought. Judge Robert was supportive to us during the interview process, saying he would welcome our questions, which gave us enough encouragement to continue. This was not the response I had expected, nor was it the response received from others.

Beginning the interview process with the judges, prosecuting attorneys, law enforcement officers, and probation department was difficult. Each department we interviewed wanted to blame another department for any problems that existed. When we interviewed the police officers/patrol officers, they'd say they picked up drunk drivers and the prosecuting attorney's office would dismiss the cases or would reduce the charges. People in the prosecuting attorney's office would say that if they "charged out" the cases, the judge would often give the offender a lenient sentence. There was a high level of inconsistency in "charging out" (we had to learn a whole new set of definitions and terminology to understand just what those in the legal/courts system were talking about) driving-while-intoxicated cases—DWIs—and in the type of sentencing the offenders received in alcohol-related cases. Probation officers complained they had far too many cases to handle, and they couldn't keep up with monitoring them all. And so it went, no one taking responsibility for leniency with DWI cases.

One unexpected result of all this was that the more time we spent interviewing, gathering statistics, and looking at the drunk-driving statistics in our community, the more comfortable we became with the process.

There wasn't much support at that time from the people we interviewed to get a MADD chapter started in Brainerd. The people we interviewed were defensive and wanted to know why we'd need a MADD chapter here. It seemed to be more of a threat to departments than an asset. The people in the departments believed that MADD was there to blame them for not doing their jobs correctly.

MADD was there, actually, to see that DWIs were prosecuted, especially when there were victims involved.

MADD began when Candy Lightner of California found out firsthand that victims were ignored in the court system, and she wanted that changed. If the various departments weren't doing their jobs, then MADD needed to push for better accountability. Regardless of the reaction we received from the people involved, Bonnie and I continued in our determination to start a chapter. The more familiar we became with the structure of the criminal justice system, the more we were determined to become chartered as a MADD chapter.

Bonnie and I could see that there were many problems regarding DWI prosecutions that we would like to see changed. We didn't want DWI charges to be reduced to careless driving; we wanted the court system to take DWIs seriously and begin prosecuting them like the crimes they were. We wanted tougher sentences than had been handed down in the past. We wanted the victims to be taken into consideration and told about the few rights they had when it could do some good during the whole punishment process.

Six months after beginning the interviews, gathering information, and discovering all we could regarding drunk driving, we became chartered as a chapter in August, 1986. MADD National had approved our paperwork and the requirements to begin a chapter. Now we were ready to inform the public what we had discovered. We notified service organizations, churches, and schools that we would be available to speak regarding Mothers Against Drunk Driving. We were given many opportunities to tell the community about MADD and what it represents.

Both Bonnie and I were drunk-driving victims, her because her children had probably ridden with their father several times while he drove drunk. We were surprised by the large number of people who had not been affected personally by drunk driving joined our

MADD chapter. That was one of the things we knew about the organization: Anyone can be a MADD member—male, female, concerned citizens, court-system personnel, victims, whoever. MADD does not turn anyone away.

One of the first speeches I gave was to the Zonta Club, an international club made up of professional women. They held their meeting at our local Elks Club during the noon hour. As I stood up to speak, I noticed the group of men at a table next to where the Zonta Club was meeting. At that table were the public defender, prosecuting attorney, and other attorneys. Yikes. How could I speak out against their DWI procedures and give statistics from our county to back up my information with them sitting right there? My first instinct was to freeze up, but I encouraged myself to get through it and not let that group intimidate me. I was supposed to inform the public of our findings regardless of who was within hearing distance. God gave me the strength to speak loudly against the practices going on in our community. First of all, I talked about the death of my daughter and the impact this had on our family. Then I explained why there was a need for MADD in our county. I began to give some of the statistics we'd gathered, such as the number of DWIs in the county and the lenient sentences that were being handed down. I informed the group about the types of cases that were being reduced to careless driving or dismissed. I told how victims were being ignored by the prosecuting attorney's office. I gave a history of MADD and mentioned what we would hoped that MADD could accomplish in making changes

None of my speaking engagements was as tough as that first one in that setting.

I thought MADD would reduce the level of anger I felt inside. I now understood the criminal justice system enough to become a victim's advocate for drunk-driving crashes—MADD says "drunk driver crashes" rather than accidents as they could be prevented and accidents are different—and I could help victims understand the legal process. This would prevent them from becoming victimized a second time by their very own justice system. I stood up in court several times and read victim impact statements for the victims because they were not emotionally able to do so themselves.

Helping other victims was rewarding for me and was the whole impetus for beginning the MADD chapter. We didn't have any control over the outcome of the cases we were involved with, but the victims felt good about knowing their rights and using them to the extent that the law would allow. Helping other victims did reduce the anger I felt inside, but it never took the anger away completely.

Chapter 10

Sharing My Pain

Compassionate Friends is a support group for parents whose children have died. In November, 1985, one of the groups started in our community. The price to pay to join this group is very high, and one that I hope others will never have to experience. You must have had a child die to belong.

It was very scary for me going to that first meeting. I had no preconceived notions about what to expect. I only knew the pain I had inside for a month was real to me, and I needed to do whatever I could do to eliminate it. There were about 20 parents whose children had died from various causes at this first meeting. The group offered support, not counseling. People shared their stories. No one was required to speak at any time during the meeting. As people introduced themselves during the meeting and told their stories, their emotions were visible. It was hard to hear all these stories at once, but also comforting knowing I wasn't alone. I vividly recall looking across the room at a mother whose son had died four years before. That woman had a smile on her face. Her smile gave me hope that I could get through my pain. I thought I'd never be able to smile again in my lifetime. Her smile gave me a ray of hope, and I held on to that. Gary only attended two or three meetings; he wanted to deal with his grief more privately. He found it hard to hear others' stories, as it would bring up his pain. It was not unusual to leave a meeting feeling worse than when you came. I attended Compassionate Friends as a member for four years and later helped facilitate the meetings.

During the times I felt I was going crazy with grief, Compassionate Friends validated that what I was feeling was normal. That validation was very important. My feelings were intense at times, but the Compassionate Friends group did not question them, nor did they try to fill me with advice. They just listened and accepted. I began to learn that being given opportunities to tell my story over and over again was crucial to my healing. Compassionate Friends became a safe haven for me to share whatever I was experiencing. The circumstances surrounding our children's deaths were individual, but the support we each received was the same.

I often felt worse after leaving the support group meeting. However, there was comfort in knowing I was not alone in my suffering, and by the next day, I would feel as if I had made some progress. There is something about sharing one's grief that helps one heal. There were many tears of pain, tears of joy, and memories shared at meetings. As time went on, I realized I could help others at Compassionate Friends' meetings.

However, rage simmered within my heart.

As with everything that is painful, recovery is a slow process. It was always hardest to be patient with myself. I expected myself to feel much better than I was. My expectations of grief were that I would share it, the pain would be reduced over time, and I could get on with my life. That was also society's expectation. Society gives people an even shorter time to recover than I gave myself. Reality had a time frame of its own, though, that far exceeded any time frame I set. I am still grieving after 21 years, but the grief no longer controls my life as it did for so many years.

During the first few months after Tammy's death, I also went to counseling, along with attending the Compassionate Friends' meetings and working on getting the MADD chapter started. There were many, many days when I simply didn't want to get up in the morning. I didn't want to face another day of my body aching from head to toe. I could get no relief from the intense physical pain I experienced each day. Whatever I tried to alleviate it was only a temporary fix, never a permanent solution.

Support from others began to taper off. I could understand that others had to get on with their lives, but I found it impossible to do the same. Life for me had changed so much that I had to begin reflecting on what life meant. My counselor suggested that I begin a journal to record my feelings. That was easier said than done. Each time I'd pick up a notebook to begin writing, the tears would begin to flow and cloud up my eyes so much I couldn't see. Eventually, however, I found that journaling my feelings became an effective way to release the many emotions I eventually experienced.

Writing down what I was feeling helped me clarify whatever I was struggling with at the time. Sometimes my thoughts were so bizarre I wondered if I were going over the edge. I didn't want to take ownership of some of those thoughts and feelings I had over the next few months. I wanted the drunk driver to be run over by another drunk driver. I wanted to inflict great pain on Richard so he would suffer as I was. I had been a compassionate, caring person before the death of my daughter, but now I had become a very angry, confused person with terrible, vengeful thoughts. This was not the me I knew. I became afraid of my own thoughts. One day I wanted to go to the cemetery and dig up Tammy's casket. I wanted to know if she was in there for real—since we never saw Tammy after her death, I now questioned if she were really dead. Thinking of digging up the casket made no sense to a rational person, but when grieving, I often lost the ability to think rationally. I called two friends, Darlene and Audrey, to come over; they did and listened to me talk about my pain that day and kept me from any rash actions. These two friends always listened compassionately to me and would act as if they had never heard the story before. Audrey and I were acquainted with each other through our children playing basketball together. Our friendship grew after each of us experienced the death of a child. Darlene's daughter, Lori, and Tammy were friends, which gave us a common bond. I am thankful that I was always able to share my feelings of heartbreak with them.

Striking revenge against Richard consumed my thinking. I wanted his house to burn down with his children in it. Only then, I figured, would he realize what pain he had inflicted on my family and me. The anger that gripped me for the people involved in the criminal justice system was equally intense. I wanted to get even with the judge who'd sentenced the defendant to just one year in jail—with a work release permit!—for the death of my loved one. I wanted to run over the prosecuting attorney and hurt him so he could begin to understand the pain I had endured. Maybe then he'd get some idea about how to work with others.

These angry thoughts scared me at times. I wasn't a violent person, and I usually didn't wish harm on anyone. One's thoughts during grieving cannot be controlled; however, we do have to take control of our actions. I was rational enough to realize that it was okay for me to have the thoughts, but I couldn't act on them. Keeping a journal was a safe way for me to release my ideas and feelings. Fortunately, I knew I would never carry out these deeds.

Admitting to anyone else that I was having these thoughts was not easy, as I felt the risk of more people finding out from those people in whom I confided. Counseling for me became my safety zone for sharing whatever I was feeling or thinking regardless of how terrible it was. It was difficult to give myself permission to accept the vengeful thoughts. When something traumatic happens, such as your child being killed, the rational thinking process is affected. I didn't like the fact that I had become capable of such violent thoughts and having such intense feelings of hatred and violence inside me.

Chapter 11

Getting Through the Holidays

The almost insurmountable task at hand now was finding a way to get through the upcoming holidays. I'd always looked forward to the holidays, but I was not joyfully anticipating the 1985 Christmas season. As I thought about Christmas, all that came to mind was that Tammy would not be with us. Thinking about the holiday was overwhelmingly depressing.

I knew that to get through the season would take some special planning, but what, and how? I had no blueprint in front of me to show me what to do or how to continue to function through this time that should be special. Christmas was a time for rejoicing, a time our family had always loved. It was a time for church, for celebrating Jesus' birthday, and a time for our extended family to get together with gifts, food, and fun. *What would this first Christmas without Tammy bring? Lord Jesus, I cannot get through this,* I thought. I want to forget Christmas and skip over to January.

I thought that perhaps shopping would ease my mind. To get my mind off Tammy, I'd go to the mall to buy gifts for others. That didn't work. Everything I saw reminded me of her. This shirt she would like. This color would look good on Tammy. She would really like this piece of jewelry. I would go home crying, unable to make any shopping decisions. *How was I going to get through buying and wrapping gifts this year?*

My husband went shopping with me one Saturday; he had a gift list for each person. He made all the decisions that year, and we completed our shopping in one day. I was thankful that he was willing to take on that task because I just couldn't make any selections.

In the past, we had always sent out Christmas cards to family and friends. This time, I couldn't think of writing or addressing cards. I couldn't bear the thought of writing about Tammy's death only three months earlier. I waited until February and sent Valentine's Day cards to everyone on our Christmas list.

We generally had our immediate family Christmas on Christmas Eve and then we went to Gary's parents' place in Bemidji, Minnesota, for Christmas Day. My mother-in-law had died on December 8, 1984, followed by my father-in-law's death on March 1, 1985. Nothing about this year's Christmas was the same as all the years before it.

We invited some of my family to be with us on Christmas Day. My mother and my sister, Lois, and her family agreed they'd come to celebrate with us. But two weeks before Christmas, they called and had to cancel. I felt crushed and devastated. We had taken such great pains to have loved ones be with us, and now for reasons of their own, my family wouldn't be here either.

It was just two weeks before Christmas, and we figured most everyone would have plans made and probably wouldn't be able to change them. *Could I make calls to other family members, or were there some friends that we could ask? Could I handle the rejection if others said no? Did I have the energy or motivation to make the phone calls at all?* This made everything more complicated and simply added to my anger.

If Tammy were alive, we wouldn't be going through this turmoil. We would have been content to be home alone. This year I needed the support and didn't think it would be good for our family to be alone. I thought we needed someone to help us through the pain of Tammy's not being with us. A diversion to our pain could help us through the day. After making calls to other family members and finding out they had plans, I thought of our neighbors across the street. I knew their children lived out of state, so there was an outside chance they'd be available. As luck would have it, Harry and Louise agreed to spend Christmas Day with us as their family would not be able to be with them. They came over in the morning and stayed with us until early evening.

We enjoyed their company and shared a great day with them. Louise introduced us to Fruit Soup as an accompaniment to our traditional turkey dinner. We ate the fruit soup as an appetizer and then sat down to a full course turkey dinner. We exchanged Christmas gifts, took pictures, and played games such as Pictionary. We talked about Tammy and what some of our other Christmases had been like. It turned out that we spent the next five Christmases with Harry and Louise. I will be forever grateful for their support and love to our family when we needed it the most.

During the times I was experiencing extensive grief, I didn't think of God as being there at all. I realize now that God was with me each and every day, whether I was consciously aware of Him or not. He was certainly aware of our needs for that first Christmas and provided for us.

Chapter 12

Anticipation of Events To Grieve

Grief has a way of coming along and tapping you on the shoulder when you least expect it. The first year after a loved one dies, there are too many first events that must be faced. The first birthday, holiday, wedding, funeral, or family gathering are tough to bear. Half of my grief work was anticipating how I'd act when the holiday or event arrived. *What would I do? How would I be affected by my grief? Could I get through this event without falling apart?* The thoughts began to pop into my mind about two weeks before any event, providing many reminders that my daughter had died and would not be a part of whatever we were doing.

The times I'd think I couldn't get through something, I'd breeze right through it without shedding a tear. Other times I'd think I can do this just fine, and before I knew it, I was in the pits. The days before that first Christmas were awful. I anticipated how dreadful the day would be. I just knew I'd spend the whole day depressed and crying. Instead, it was such a relief when the day finally came that I was able to pass the time without too much difficulty. I would never have thought that possible.

The Saturday before Easter, we drove to Bemidji to spend the weekend with Gary's sister, Mary Kay, and her family. I didn't think that would be too difficult. On Easter morning, I woke up with my emotions a mess, totally depressed. I couldn't explain what I was feeling, but I knew I needed to go home. Fortunately, my husband supported me, and we packed up the family before dinner and drove home. My grief was always unpredictable, and this time it surfaced when I least expected it.

Tammy would have graduated from high school in May, 1986. How would I ever be able to get through that time? Tammy had talked about graduation and what she wanted to do afterward. I knew that receiving graduation invitations in the mail would trigger some intense pain. I was so angry and felt so cheated at not being able to be part of Tammy's graduation.

As I read my journal entries regarding graduation, I realize how intense my rage was:

May 9: "I am so angry at that drunk driver. I could send him a graduation invitation with a picture of a casket in it. I feel like choking him for what he has done to my family. I looked forward to Tammy's graduation for so long. We talked about it many times and used to joke about how then she would be strictly on her own and wouldn't have to listen to me anymore. While others are planning a graduation open house, I feel empty since I have nothing to plan. I could be sending out invitations, baking cookies, wondering how to decorate the house, and working on all the details that would go into making a big celebration for a long-anticipated occasion. Instead, I feel pain and cry buckets of tears."

May 23: "Tammy, today I am thinking of you and visiting your grave site instead of planning your graduation party. I know intellectually that you are at peace and have met your goals in life. I get angry knowing you were able to do that without me. You do not have to go through any more pain and frustrations as I do and am faced with every day. Graduation is one week away, and I will miss seeing you enjoy the ceremony. It is difficult not being able to see you walk proudly down the aisle to receive your well-deserved diploma. This Saturday at your Cousin Shelly's graduation, I will be thinking of you and feeling the loss. There are so many reminders of you each day. The love I have for you keeps flowing, so I am using the energy from that love in ways that I know how. Working hard for MADD to get drunk drivers off the highway is one way I use up that extra energy. I love you and continue to be your mother, and I think of you often each day."

May 27: "Spending Memorial Day with your daughter at the cemetery is the pits. I get so angry thinking about the tragic way she died and had her life stolen from us. It would be so easy to sleep the next few days away. I could be planning a graduation party and looking forward to seeing Tammy receive her diploma. I feel anger, rage, pain, and frustration. I feel helpless in knowing how to get through this time. I have looked forward to seeing Tammy graduate, and that piece of joy was stolen from me. Anger and hatred is all I feel. I want to be able to be proud of Tammy's friends as they graduate, but all I feel is loss and pain. What should be one of the happiest times to experience as a parent is going to be painful and sad."

I did attend the graduation ceremonies at the high school. I sat in the back, filled with emptiness. Tears streamed down my face throughout the event. I had so many mixed emotions. I was happy for Tammy's friends who were graduating, even though many of them were also grieving the loss of their friend and classmate. After graduation, I congratulated Tammy's friends. They shared with me how they also missed Tammy being in the graduation ceremony. Afterward, I immediately went to the car and fell into tears. I can look back at graduation, however, and say, "Yes, I did get through one more thing without Tammy's presence."

About two weeks before the anniversary of Tammy's death, I began to experience a lot of anxiety. The date of her *crash would soon be arriving. How would I handle the 13th of September, 1986?*

How would I get through this day when it arrived? The crash details began to replay daily in my mind. *What would I do on the 13th? How should I act? What would be the least painful way to endure that horrible anniversary? Would others remember the date? Should I talk about the crash and remind others, or should I just remain quiet so others wouldn't feel uncomfortable?* I just wanted the day to come and go. I didn't want to face dealing with another bad day. *How could I plan ahead to avoid being totally depressed and wiped out?* These questions swirled round and round, torturing me, especially as I had no answers to any of them.

This was another of those times when my rage was simply out of control. Grief was a great deal of work. So much of my time and energy was being wasted because of the crash that took the life of my precious daughter. If she hadn't been killed, I wouldn't be going through all this. Feeling sorry for myself was a new concept for me, but one with which I began to become all-too familiar. Just when I'd have a few days in succession when I was gaining some strength and getting control over my grief, those feelings erupted and began all over again. Tears consumed many hours of my day. I relived over and over all that had happened from the time of being notified of my daughter's death.

When the day finally arrived, it was almost a relief. I spent time at the cemetery. We received some "Thinking of you" cards from friends and family. Several people called to ask how I was and to say they remembered the day too. It was both heartwarming and surprising that so many people remembered the date.

The anticipation of the day was much worse than the actual day. I figured I could now get on with my life. It was such a relief to get the first year of grieving behind me. I thought that now my life would start to settle down and get back to normal—whatever normal was. I soon found out there is no such thing as normal. What was normal to me before now had to be redefined. What was normal before was never again to be a part of my life. Normal was a word that had no meaning.

Chapter 13

Mourning, How Long?

I was surprised and disappointed that I still had so many bad days. On those rotten days, I had no energy, no desire to do anything, and no motivation. I just had a deep longing for my daughter and to recapture my old life.

My pain seemed to travel to a deeper level. I hadn't expected a second year of grieving. I had expected the pain to be reduced, not increased. I did not think the second year of mourning was going to be as bad as, and certainly not worse than, the first. I had heard the second year of grieving was often worse than the first, but I didn't want to believe that.

The questions still blew in to haunt me. *How long, Lord? How long must I feel this pain, this deep longing? What could fill up that emptiness?* I began to think there would never be better days ahead and that I'd never feel at peace again. The best I could do each day was to get up in the morning and not expect too much from myself. I couldn't control or change what I was feeling. I never expected my grief to be so intense. I never expected to feel as if my life were over. I never expected to be so depressed and to have so many dark and negative feelings. There are no other words that can describe grief than "the pits." *How do I get out of the pits?* I could see no way out. I did the best I could each day, but most days that did not seem good enough.

I knew I'd better start finding a way to accept what had happened.

I didn't like my life and all that grief brought with it. There were very few happy moments and not much laughter. Gary, Jennifer, and Jeff wanted me to feel better, to be involved, to get on with life, but I couldn't find a strategy to do that. I did a lot of pretending to others that I was doing better than I was. What was going on inside of me emotionally wasn't what I wanted to show to others; what others saw and what I felt were not the same. I tried to be what others wanted me to be. I tried to present myself in the way that I thought others expected me to be.

I spent many hours each day home alone, just staring into space. My purpose in life was lost. Most days had no meaning for me. I began to think I could not go on like this anymore. *Help me, someone, help me I wanted to cry. Whom else could I talk to? Who would best understand?* A year had passed since Tammy's death. I knew I should have overcome these feelings by now. *What was wrong with me? Would this pain ever end?* I couldn't get control of my emotions. I hated how my life was going. I wasn't a negative person, but everything about me felt negative. *Stop! Stop! No more!* I needed to do something different, but what?

No matter what I did, there was always the underlying depression. During the first year after Tammy was killed, I tried to function as a mother to Jeff and Jennifer. A couple of weeks after the funeral, Gary and I went to school to hear Jennifer audition for sixth-grade band. I wanted to be there for her, but my mind was preoccupied with grief. I was interested in what instrument she would play for band but couldn't show my usual enthusiasm. Here was something else Richard had robbed me of—being able to enjoy my other children.

I tried to be involved with Jeff and Jennifer's activities, but I felt like a robot going through the motions. Jeff played on the sophomore basketball team. Even though I often felt like sitting home to be alone with my grief, we went to all his games. I enjoyed watching him play, but it was only a temporary reprieve from mourning. Tammy had been a basketball player, and going to Jeff's games was bittersweet; the games reminded me that Tammy would never again play the game she loved. Enjoying family activities and being "in the moment" at events was a challenge, but I tried. Once it was over, the grief returned like a rushing tide. I could find no escape from it.

Many months still found me anticipating how my grief would flood my heart following some joyful event, making the activity itself almost an afterthought.

Tammy's 19th birthday was approaching on October 19th. My reaction was almost exactly like the one the year before. *What should I do? How was I supposed to act?* I couldn't just ignore the day. *Could I bake her a cake without everyone thinking I'd gone crazy?* We had to have some sort of celebration on her birthday. *Lord, why am I still struggling with this so much?* I couldn't even give myself permission to bake a cake. It shouldn't be such an ordeal, but it was. *Had anyone but me struggled with making a cake on a deceased one's birthday?* I decided to bake a cake; I didn't care if it was abnormal. I had to do that one little thing in Tammy's memory. *Would anyone else remember her birthday?* I baked a big double-layer chocolate cake and felt pleased and relieved. My family accepted the cake and didn't think I was foolish. The biggest challenge had been the struggle to give myself permission to do something that didn't make sense. It seemed important to follow my gut instinct, regardless of what others might say or think about the situation. Eventually, listening to my gut instinct would be one key to my finding inner peace.

During this stage of the mourning process, I reflected back to the state of my emotions two years ago, and I realized I was making progress. *My tearful outbursts aren't as intense and have dwindled to wider intervals.* Tears are healing, so I figured with all the tears I shed, there must be some healing going on somewhere. Identifying the progress I was making wasn't easy, of course, as I still felt consumed with mourning. The process was frustrating, and I often thought I was going backwards rather than forward. I wasn't being gentle with myself. I set an unreachable standard for myself, thinking I should be progressing at a greater rate. I knew I never would get over my daughter's brutal death completely, but I hoped I could find ways to live with it and reconcile the pain.

My hands and feet began to hurt in December 1988. Walking would shoot pain throughout my foot. The suffering was intense, almost unbearable. I couldn't use blankets at night because it hurt to have my hands or legs touch anything. Some days both problems tormented me: I couldn't use my hands, and I could hardly walk. I was frightened. I went to a doctor and was diagnosed with Rheumatoid Arthritis. *How could I have this illness?* I was only 45 years old! Arthritis was for older people, not for me. The doctor recommended some medication to reduce the swelling, but it wasn't that effective. I went to an arthritis specialist and began taking hot wax treatments on my hands three times a week. What a nuisance it was for me to have to give up time three times a week to go for treatments. It made no sense to me that while I still suffered from grief, now I was afflicted with an incurable illness. I did, however, receive the hot wax treatments as recommended. I'd go to the clinic and dip my hands in this warm wax, and then my hands would be wrapped in a towel for a period of time. After the wax was peeled off my hands, the swelling went down, and the pain was livable. The pain was never completely gone, but it was manageable. I was now taking 12 aspirin a day to reduce the swelling and eliminate the pain.

I had to learn to deal with the physical pain of arthritis as well as the emotional pain of mourning. Many days I could not do much of anything. My fingers swelled bigger than sausages. To touch anything was very painful. Evidently, I would have to learn to live with taking aspirin and hot wax treatments the rest of my life. I asked myself, *haven't I suffered too much already to now be afflicted with physical pain on top of my emotional pain?* The book of Job became my friend as I could truly relate to Job's adversity.

Chapter 14

Anger Takes Its Toll

Whenever I thought about our legal system and what they call justice, anger overpowered me. Because my daughter's death was so traumatic, the intensity of my anger was frightening. Even the word rage doesn't describe the fury I harbored. Hateful thoughts ate at me all day long. It began to affect almost everything I did. I was short and snappy with comments to my family. I had wild bursts of anger inappropriate to what was going on at the time. I'd "fly off the handle" at a sales clerk for no reason. My voice had a harsh and edgy tone to it. I went berserk whenever I heard of someone getting killed by a drunk driver. I had a steady, pounding anger inside me constantly. There seemed to be no way to release this anger so it wouldn't return. Anger began to control me, to consume me, and to overshadow my whole being.

One way I found to deal with my molten fury was through writing. The following excerpts from my journals show the intensity of the anger seething inside my heart:

"Richard ought to be hung by his toenails."

"I wish the defense attorney and the prosecuting attorney would both lose one of their kids, and maybe then they would understand what they do to people and especially what they did to me."

"The prosecuting attorney has no awareness of how someone feels after losing a child in a crash by a drunk driver. He is going to find out as I am going to let him know. His wishy-washy ways of handling cases better change, or he's going to lose his job. I'll take the risk of being sued for slander before I let him get by with what he's doing."

"He is such a @#$*^% that he doesn't have the guts to ask for justice."

"When I see the prosecuting attorney, I want to slam him in the face or run him over. Would that wake him up?"

"Losing Tammy is very traumatic to me, and I will not stand the justice system making a mockery of the whole situation. I will not stop until I have been heard."

"How can that judge stand up there on his pedestal and talk about how he doesn't believe in drunk driving? He says the person should be punished, and his court won't stand for this. He wants to make an impression on society. He can say all this garbage out of his mouth and then take it all back by sentencing a murderer to one year in the county jail on the work-release system. It doesn't make sense to me how he can be such a hypocrite and then be able to look himself in the mirror each morning."

"I'd like to punch the defense attorney's lights out and then walk by and laugh, saying, 'I should be queen for the day because I have suffered too much for the cruelty I did to him.' Maybe then he could realize how he slapped my face in the courtroom. He doesn't know what suffering is. His life is obviously too easy, and he hasn't felt any pain."

"Richard murdered my daughter, and he should pay for it. I want to run him over. What pain has he felt? I do not feel he has felt anything yet. He certainly hasn't suffered any pain from what the judge gave him."

"The whole justice system seems to be stuck together like glue. Well, he killed the wrong person, and I won't stop until changes have been made. No one should have to be treated like nothing in the court process."

After experiencing these kind of thoughts each day, I now had the problem of figuring out what to do with the anger. That was the most difficult and painful part. I was angry at many things, and most of the time my distress was unexplainable. Anger was just with me. I could get angry because someone "looked" at me. I could get angry because of comments like, "You still have two other children," or "God must have wanted your daughter." These remarks sent me off the deep end. I got angry just because I had to get up in the morning and had to face another day. I was angry because my life had turned upside down, and every day was filled with tears and pain. I was angry because other people were happy and laughing and appeared to be having fun. I was angry because Jeff and Jennifer had to go through life without their sister whom they loved so deeply.

Anger made my life miserable. I couldn't find a way to release it for it to be gone completely. Each time I did something to free it, like writing in my journal or discussing it with someone, I'd feel better temporarily. But then it slowly crept back. I could not get rid of it. I could not find the answer.

Reading the book of Job in the Good News Bible helped. Job tells the story of a man who has accomplished much in his life and has a lot of money, a big family, and is healthy and of a sound of mind. Job was a good person who tried to be righteous. He had a strong faith and believed in God and who God was. He was a man of prayer and counted on God to be there for him. Then, Job lost everything he had—his wealth, his possessions, and his family.

Job begins to grieve, to be angry, and to lose control of his security. His friends come to comfort him, but instead give him a lot of unwelcome advice. Job does not receive most of the advice well. Job 3:11 states, "I wish I had died in my mother's womb or died the moment I was born." Job 3:26 says, "I have no peace, no rest, and my troubles never end." I could relate to the pain that Job experienced. Job 9:25-28 reads, "My day's race by, not one of them good. My life passes like the swiftest boat, as fast as an eagle swooping down on a rabbit. If I smile and try to forget my pain, all my suffering comes back to haunt me."

As I read those verses, I said to myself, "That is exactly how I feel. Life is passing me by, and I am in too much pain to enjoy it. My suffering does not end."

Regardless of all the pain and suffering Job went through, underneath it all, he held onto his faith. He never lost his love for God. He was still able to pray, but he often felt as if God was not listening to his prayers. Job realized that only God could replace his answer with peace. I found that comforting, and it helped me to realize that what I experienced was normal.

I had always felt I had a personal relationship with the Lord Jesus, and I prayed regularly. The church meant a great deal to me, and I still attended church faithfully every Sunday. I often went to church during the week. I taught a class, I was active in a women's group, and I worked at various church activities. I was a member of the Council of Catholic Women and had served on the board in several capacities. I kept busy to avoid feeling constant pain.

During the third year after dealing with my grief and not feeling as if I'd made progress, I'd begun to question my faith. *Why? Why? Why?* That seemed to be the question that came to me the most. I wasn't able to say, *Why not? What was God trying to teach me through this suffering? Was there a lesson for me? Had I not been a good enough mother? Was I being punished? Didn't I pray enough? What sins had I committed for which I was being punished? Is it okay to be angry with God? Will He love me again if I let out my anger toward Him? What do I do to get through this pain? Will I ever experience peace again? How and what do I pray for now? God said He would not give me more than I can handle, but do I believe that? I know this pain is more than I can handle. So now what? I do not think I will ever find inner peace or a meaningful relationship with God again. But how can I think like that? There must be something wrong with me.*

Again, the questions just wouldn't stop. All questions, but no answers. *Would there ever be answers? When? How long would I have to wait before I could sort all this out?*

After going to church every Sunday for three years after Tammy's death, I often wondered if I could find meaning in the church again. One day the tears spilled down my cheeks for almost the whole hour during Mass. I felt sorry for anyone who sat near me because I wore my feelings on the outside for everyone to see. I couldn't hold them back, though; they were stronger than I was.

The songs we sang each Sunday almost tore me apart inside since many were ones we'd sung at Tammy's funeral. I could only cry. At times my body would shake from the intense pain that was being triggered inside me just from hearing the song "Be Not Afraid," "On Eagle's Wings," and "Here I Am, Lord."

Gary tried to comfort me.

My children were embarrassed because their mom was crying during church.

I thought, *how long, Lord, how long will I feel like this? When will I ever be able to go to church and get something out of it? Should I just stop going to church?* I knew I couldn't do that, but I thought it many times.

In the past, I always looked forward to going to Mass on Sundays, but now I actually dreaded going because it seemed to bring my pain right to the surface.

Chapter 15

Searching for an Answer

We never know how one experience on any given day can be the beginning of a healing process months later. That experience may be the answer for which you have been looking. For me, that day was in January, 1989.

One morning during that month I was in total despair. I was sick and tired of being in the pits. I wanted my pain to end. I didn't want any more of this grieving stuff. I was crying that day as if it were the beginning of my grieving, not almost four years later. I was depressed and feeling sorry for myself. After grieving for three years and three months, I couldn't take one more day of feeling this intense sadness, depression, and hopelessness.

I thought about committing suicide. I was frightened by that. I had no suicide plan, and I don't think I would have ever carried one out, but the fact that I had such a heavy black cloud of despair over my head more than three years after Tammy's death was disheartening. I couldn't understand why I wasn't getting over it. *Why wasn't I able to get my act together?* I was beginning to withdraw from others and isolate myself. I wouldn't reach out to others. I found excuses not to attend meetings or events. I felt as if I had nothing for which to live. I was in such intense pain. Thinking about how my family would feel without me never entered my mind. I was too consumed with my own pain to think about others. Looking in the mirror, I saw this pitiful sight of myself with such hopelessness. My eyes were red from crying. My face had no color. I had the look of a person in despair.

I called out to the Lord, "Lord, you had better give me the name of a person I can talk to before I do something crazy."

Immediately, the name of Father Con came to mind. My first reaction was to say, "No way am I going to call Father Con."

He was new to our parish and had arrived at church after Tammy's death, so he didn't know much about her or the crash. I couldn't call him. *What would I say?* But his name kept getting stronger and stronger in my mind. I was feeling desperate. I had called out to God, and He had not given me the answer I wanted.

I ignored this inner prompting. I went to the phone and called Audrey. No answer. I cried for a time and tried another friend. No answer. By now, I was sinking in my grief. I knew I had to do something. Finally, I called Father Con. He answered the phone. *How often does a priest himself answer the phone?* I told him I was in a lot of pain and needed someone to listen to me. He said he had time to listen, and I could come right over to the church. I began to feel guilty because I called out to God for help, He had offered me help, and my first response had been to ignore Him and to fight what He was offering me.

Somehow, I pulled myself together and drove across town to visit Father Con at church. He listened attentively as I told my story of how Tammy had died, the mourning I was still suffering through, and how desperate I was feeling that day. He let me pour my heart out and babble my words through the tears.

After I finished telling my story, Father Con asked me if I would consider going on a retreat—an eight-day "silent" retreat. I would be assigned a director I could meet with one hour a day. The rest of the day would be spent in silence with God. This was a retreat for people working in the ministry, but lay people were allowed to attend.

I didn't understand how a retreat could be an answer for me, but I was so desperate I would have agreed to most anything that day. I had tried everything I knew to relieve my pain, but nothing had worked. It was easy to agree to attend a retreat in June. After all, it was only January, and the retreat was months away. Even though I had six months before the retreat, it was something safely far enough away in time.

I left the church office feeling better that I now had a plan. I could look forward to an event on my calendar—an eight-day silent retreat with others who were in ministry. *Could this be the answer I was looking for?* I had no answer to that question. All I knew for sure was that God did have His hand in this plan.

After I had agreed to attend the silent retreat, Father Con often sought me out to talk about the retreat. He was so excited that I was going. He told me he had attended several retreats and felt especially close to God during those times. I knew he wanted that for me, but I had no hope for that happening. He told me to bring along my Bible but no other reading material. I was to be free to focus on God and what He would say to me. I was to spend my time listening to God and not take other reading materials along to distract me. Being alone with God and my Bible for eight days seemed intimidating. As a person whose mind often raced 100 miles per hour a day, how could I be silent during this retreat? *What would I do all day long? How would I be able to let go of my thoughts and feelings enough to allow God to be fully in charge?* I felt the retreat was what I was supposed to do, but I certainly had many questions about how I could accomplish it.

My depression wasn't so intense during the six months from January to June 1989. It never disappeared, but I was able to cope better, knowing I had a plan to do something. But the closer June approached, the more anxious I became. I had to keep telling myself I could do it. Going to the retreat could not be as bad as living the way I'd been living for three and a half years.

Chapter 16

Silent Retreat Day 1—Anxiety

The day in June finally arrived. My bag in one hand, my Bible in the other, I set out in my little red car for a three-hour drive to the Dunrovin Retreat Center, north of Stillwater, Minnesota. I turned off the radio on the way to my destination and drove in silence. I began to realize I had not spent huge chunks of time in silence before. When I was home alone, I often had the television on or music playing. I was seldom in complete silence.

Apprehension about what the next days would bring began to surface. More than once, I thought, *I do not have to do this. I can turn around and be a no-show at this retreat.* But then I'd think of Father Con and what he'd think if I didn't go, so I continued. I didn't want to disappoint him.

For whom was I going to this silent retreat? I asked myself. *Father Con or me?* It was pretty evident that at this point that I was more concerned with Father Con's opinion of me than I was with this opportunity to spend time with God.

While I drove, I replayed in my mind all of the details of the night Tammy died. I relived the planning of her funeral. All the days and years of grieving that I thought I was working through bubbled up inside of me. I basically relived what I had experienced during the past three and three quarters years. I was surprised at how much I remembered. The three-hour drive went by rather quickly.

When I drew near the retreat center, I saw the little white sign on the side of the road that said "Dunrovin," with an arrow pointing left. Here I was. There could be no turning back now; I had arrived at Dunrovin, the place I had been waiting to go to since January. *I have to do this*, I kept reassuring myself. I put on my car blinker to turn left onto a path of many unknowns.

The minute I turned off the busy highway and onto the narrow, wooded road to Dunrovin, I began to sense the silence. It was deafening. I cannot remember a time when I was so aware of an absence of noise. I wasn't prepared for it. I had too many fears and questions inside me to recognize the gift I was receiving. That half-mile drive to the parking lot seemed longer than the three hours I had just completed to this point.

I pulled into the parking lot, shut off the car, took a deep breath, and said a short prayer, "Lord, give me the strength to follow through with this retreat."

Directly across from the parking lot was a pond surrounded by trees. A walking path went around the pond. The scene was absolutely beautiful. The quiet, serene setting had a calming effect. I began to settle down inside, the anxiety level lessening a notch.

After entering the building, I walked down a long hallway past several doors that I assumed would be my living quarters for the next eight days. At the end of the hallway was a big living area on one side with a dining room on the other. No people were in sight.

Had I arrived too early? How would I register? How would I find out my room number? There was no one to greet me, and I wondered if I were in the right place. Finally, off to the side I noticed a sign that said, "Register Here." There was a sheet of paper with room numbers listed on it. All I needed to do was put my name beside a room number and take my belongings to that room. The usual registration table and long lines to sign in were missing; there was only more silence. *What had I gotten myself into?*

I put my name beside room number 104 and went to investigate it. Opening a door to a long hallway reminded me of my college dormitory. I found room 104. The door was open. I peeked inside and saw a bed, a built-in table that I assumed would be a desk, a chair, a lamp, a sink, and a closet. The room was adequate but small, and did not come with a soft, easy chair to lounge around in, only the bare necessities. This would be my home for the next eight days.

At this point, I knew two things: one, my director was Brother Bill, and two, everyone was to gather at 7:00 p.m. upstairs in the chapel. The participants were mostly priests, a few sisters, two other lay persons, and four directors from Loyola. It was now about 6:45 p.m. I looked over the place, found where I needed to be, and surveyed the grounds. The surroundings could not have been more perfect. The Saint Croix River flowed along the east side of the property. A peaceful-looking pond featured birds chirping everywhere. There was even an outdoor swimming pool. If I had not had to think about my pain and anxiety, Dunrovin would have been a perfect setting for rest and relaxation—nothing too fancy, just quiet and serene.

Everything inside me was beginning to churn, actually. On the outside, I probably looked cool and confident. No one could see the clammy, sweaty palms of my hands. The unknown, which lie ahead, was scaring me half to death.

The first person I met at the retreat was Carolyn from Duluth. She drove up and parked while I was outside observing the grounds. Carolyn told me she had been on many retreats in the past and made me feel welcome. She was handicapped and in a wheelchair, and it felt good to help someone in need since it took my mind off my anxiety.

As I arrived in the big room that would serve as our chapel

area where we were to gather to receive the agenda for the week, I was feeling really lost. I hoped that no one would notice how uncomfortable I was. Father Dick came up to me and introduced himself. After I told him my name, he said, "I'm so glad you are here, and I'm glad to meet you." He asked if he could give me a hug. I accepted graciously and again felt welcome. He was in charge of the retreat. I wondered what Father Con had told him about me. I now felt as if my pain was written all over me in both my body language and my facial expression.

The Dunrovin personnel, Brother James and Brother Lawrence, introduced themselves and welcomed the twenty-four of us to Dunrovin. Then it was time for more introductions. We were all sitting in chairs that formed a circle. We were to go around the room and say our name, the name of our church, and if we wanted, any special prayer request.

When it came to my turn, I said, "I am Pat Bluth; I attend St. Andrews Church in Brainerd." Tears abruptly streamed down my face as I added, "And I need a lot of prayer." I didn't think I was going to be able to say any more, but I took a deep breath and said, "I am here for healing, grieving, and dealing with how angry I am." I couldn't say anything else because if I did, I would have completely fallen apart.

I was unprepared for the pain that had risen to the surface so quickly. It took me awhile to regain my composure. I had nothing to wipe my eyes with, so tears were dripping down my cheeks. I wanted to leave the room and go have a good cry. Remembering anyone's name at this time was impossible, as was making note of his or her prayer requests. Hardly anything sank into my brain during that meeting. I did remember that one person, a nun, was having chemotherapy treatments and wanted prayers for healing. Most of the others were seeking a deeper, inner peace. I was thinking that any kind of inner peace would be welcome.

Then we sang "Come, Holy Ghost" and read Psalm 139, which was to be our Scripture to reflect on during the week:

O Lord, you have probed me and you know me; you know when I sit and when I stand; you understand my thoughts from afar. My journeys and my rest you scrutinize, with all my ways you are familiar. Where can I go from your spirit? From your presence, where can I flee? If I go up to the heavens, you are there; if I sink to the netherworld, you are present there.

Each participant had been assigned a director upon pre-registration. We divided up and met with our director and the others he would be directing. My director was Brother Bill, a Christian brother. Brother Bill had worked in Peru and had planned on returning there soon. The only other person he would direct other than me was a lady named Marge. We were the only two on retreat who were not priests or nuns. When we met for the first time, the tears wouldn't stop dripping down my cheeks. I found it hard to concentrate. We were to schedule a time each day that we would meet with our director for one hour. That one hour meeting was the only time we could talk. Otherwise, complete silence was expected. We were to spend our time in prayer, reading Scripture, or listening. I was scheduled to meet with Brother Bill at 9:00 each morning.

Our schedule for the day went like this: Breakfast at 8:00 a.m., lunch at noon, Mass at 5:00 p.m., and dinner at 6:00 p.m. Aside from the one-hour session with our director, the rest of the time was ours to spend with God.

Before excusing us the first evening, Brother Bill suggested we try to use imagery. I was to imagine sitting on a bleacher in the person's lap behind me, or sitting on the lawn having fallen into someone's lap. Now, I was to imagine that it was God's lap in which I was sitting. At this point in the retreat, I could not allow myself to do that. My reaction surprised me; I would have thought that I could have leaned into God's lap and relaxed there. I hoped that I could find enough peace to just let go and let God hold me like Brother Bill described. It sounded like something I would certainly enjoy at some point in my life down the road. For tonight, it was not going to happen. After having been given that assignment, we were excused for the evening.

I could do whatever I wanted for the rest of the evening. My first reaction was to pack up and go home. I did not want to stay one more second. This was not for me. It was too scary and emotionally uncomfortable being on retreat. Back in my room, tears just poured out of me. It seemed that all my pain from almost four years had been again released. Since I had been crying on and off for that amount of time, I was surprised by the flood of more tears. I didn't think I had that many tears left in me.

Trying to regain my composure, I told myself that I couldn't sit around crying all the time. I decided to go outside and take a walk. Perhaps some fresh air would do me some good. My tears just kept coming. I finally succumbed to the tears, sat down on a bench outside, and sobbed. The pain inside me wanted to be released. It was so intense that I couldn't hold it back. I realized that the pain stored up inside me was preventing me from finding any inner peace. It had been a long time since I had allowed myself to cry this intently and for such a long time. The intensity of the pain I felt that first night was as strong as the first weeks after Tammy's death. It seemed to engulf my whole being.

I was looking for any excuse to justify packing up and going home. I wondered if Brother Bill was the right director for me. I told myself I must have faith that God was the one in control. I prayed to God to help keep me open to whatever His plan for me was. By the time I went to bed that night, I was totally exhausted, but I had not run away. It would have been very easy for me to run away if I hadn't cared about disappointing Father Con.

Chapter 17

Retreat Day 2—Telling My Story and Finding a New Image of God

Breakfast in silence was a unique experience. Six people sat at each table. Sitting at a table with others and not being able to talk was very uncomfortable. Meal time to me had always been a time to converse, a time to find out about each other, and to share one's plans for the day. I was curious to meet everyone and find out more about them. Father Con had warned me of the challenge of quieting down one's mind to get into complete silence. My insides were screaming out to talk. My mind kept focusing on how uncomfortable it was to sit in complete silence and to wonder what other people were thinking. Was I the only one uncomfortable with that?

Could I put my judgments aside long enough to work with Brother Bill, and let God be in control? I didn't see that I had any other choice. At 9:00 a.m., after breakfast, I met with Brother Bill and began to tell him my story. I explained how my daughter had died so senselessly because of a drunk driver. I was surprised how deep my pain was and how easily it flowed out. I was an emotional wreck, trudging down a path I didn't want to go down again. My anger toward God resurfaced. I was angry because I knew He had the power to stop the crash and prevent her from dying. I had not realized how angry I really was at God.

Telling my story to Brother Bill meant reliving it. Some of the painful events that had taken place after Tammy's death resurfaced. I remembered how awful it was knowing that Tammy was dead and not being able to say goodbye because other people had decided Tammy's body was too badly damaged for me to see. My anger at those other people making decisions for me that weren't what I wanted erupted. I was angry with God for the violent way Tammy died. She did not deserve to burn beyond recognition. I understand that God lets people suffer the consequences for their own actions, but Tammy was not doing anything wrong. She just happened to be in the path of a drunk driver. It did not seem fair to me that Tammy had to pay such a deadly price for someone else's actions.

I could understand all this in my head, but it did not help my heart, and it certainly did not ease the pain I felt. I wanted to find a way to let go of this pain and not to let it continue to control my life. I think I had accepted that Tammy was dead, but I had not accepted the violent way she died. My beautiful 17-year-old daughter dying of fourth-degree burns, which made her unrecognizable, was more than I could bear to deal with. I told Brother Bill the questions with which I often wrestled, *What did she feel? How did she look after being burned? Was there anything left of her? Would I find these answers during this time at retreat? Where was the hope I needed?* Hope began to fade and helplessness began to take over again right then in Brother Bill's office.

Forgiveness was a big issue with me. I realized that not forgiving could be blocking my growth, and it could be a big cause of my arthritis. I struggled with knowing what forgiveness meant. *If I forgive, does that mean all is okay and that everything is all right? Does it mean that this death never happened? If so, then I didn't want to forgive. Does forgiveness mean everything should be all right now? If I* could define what forgiveness meant to me, maybe then and only then, I would be able to forgive God and the drunk driver. Being able to forgive was way beyond my comprehension right then. Only a miracle would cause me to forgive.

Brother Bill asked me to open up my image of God. He suggested I might be seeing Him in a scary, powerful position, an image that might be too big. I needed to expand my image of God through prayer and not to be so rigid and closed in my thinking. He asked me to reflect on Isaiah 49:13-16:

Sing out, O heavens, and rejoice, O earth,
Break forth into song, you mountains.
For the Lord comforts his people
And shows mercy to his afflicted.

But Zion said, "The Lord has forsaken me;
My Lord has forgotten me."

Can a Mother forget her infant,
be without tenderness for the child of her womb?
Even should she forget,
I will never forget you.

See, upon the palms of my hands
I have written your name;
your walls are ever before me.

I prayed, "God, I am asking for your help in giving me a new image of You. One that will not be so scary and powerful. I need an image that will help me process the grief I am experiencing. I need help in learning how to forgive. This image of You will help me with the many questions surrounding Tammy's death. I hope the image will help me understand the senselessness of the whole crash and how Tammy died.

"Lord, I am struggling with being angry with You and how to get beyond that anger. Last night I was asked to let You hold me in an imagery exercise, and I was afraid to let go. What am I afraid to let go of? If I let go, does that mean I have forgiven You, even if I am not ready for that yet?

"Help me to understand the confusion I feel about loving You and hating You. Lord, I know you are important in my life, but how can I love You and still be so angry with you?

"Tammy was going to make a retreat and ask you into her life. She never got that chance because the night before, you took her away from me. Is she with You? I would like to know that You took her soul and her spirit, and that she is happy with You. Does her burning to death take that away?"

"Is there any sign that you can give me, Lord, that will let me know Tammy is in Your arms safe and happy? Do I need to know that to have peace for myself? Lord, I need Your love and some answers."

I was filled with pain. There was no room for positive thoughts. It occurred to me that writing out my thoughts, feelings, and prayers could help me put some perspective to my confusion.

My conversation with God continued, "Talking about and thinking about the pain so much makes me feel like a broken record regarding Tammy's death. I've tried all the ways I know to handle the pain. I've talked about it until I am blue in the face. I've written about it. I shared it in support group. I cried about it. I was silent about it. Nothing has taken the pain away.

"Lord, I want to dump this pain on You and let You take it. I have had it for almost four long years, and that is enough. I am ready to let go and quit hanging on to the pain. Why do I need all this pain? I don't. Lord, please take the pain from me so I can get unstuck and begin to grow spiritually. I know You are big enough to handle all my pain. Won't You embrace the pain and help me get beyond it? A statement from Father Dick keeps playing in my mind. He says that when you pray, pray big. So that is what I am doing.

"Lord, I am praying really big. This pain is much too big for me to handle. My heart is heavy laden. I would like to have an empty heart that can be filled with joy, forgiveness, and love—not a heart overwhelmed with pain and anger. Lord, I am giving You the pain I am feeling now, and I expect You to accept it."

After praying to God to help me find a better image of Him, the answer to that prayer began to come. The answer wasn't instant, but it did become clear during the same day I prayed. I began to have positive, not angry thoughts about God. I was not sure I wanted to write down these new thoughts about God. If they were true, then that brought about a new set of questions. *How could a positive, good, loving God have allowed the gruesome death of my daughter? How could He have allowed such a cruel way for her to die? When will I get answers*, I wondered, *and not so many questions?*

Father Con never promised the week with God would be easy. I knew I needed to quit fighting the process and allow it to flow. So I began to write out the new image of God that was coming into my mind.

God is sensitive. The day of Tammy's funeral, I remember there was a light mist all day long. It did not really rain, just a steady mist. God was crying with me, and those were His tears.

God loves and cares. I know He is the one behind my being at this retreat. If He did not care, He would not keep opening doors for me to get to know Him better.

God can forgive. Because of my hatred and anger toward God, He can put that aside and still show me love. That is a good sign of forgiveness.

God is patient. He has given me a lot of time to work and process my pain. After nearly four long years since Tammy's death, He still has not given up on me. Even though I have shut the door on God, the door never locks. The door always reopens easily.

God is present with me. I can certainly feel His presence working within me today. The words just seem to flow out. I only have to listen to Him. Is this what Brother Bill means by "testing out the image"?

God listens. I know He has heard my prayer today. The answer to my prayer is evident as this new image of God appears in my thoughts.

God is in charge and in control if I can let go and let it happen. I know these are God's words that are being put down here today. I have not experienced these thoughts since Tammy's death. My thoughts have been so negative and filled with anger that I could not have gotten in touch with these positive thoughts on my own.

Later that day, I walked into the chapel. There was a library there. A book that caught my eye was *Mary, the Perfect Prayer Partner.* Another answer to prayer seemed to leap out at me as I paged through the book. The answer to some of my questions was submission. "Let it be. Not my will but thine be done." Mary was the first to say those words. We can use Mary as a model in saying yes to God. No matter what life demands of me, it will be easier to handle if I submit to God in faith and trust.

The second day of retreat was a roller-coaster ride. My mind was so busy with thoughts that I felt like I was talking to someone every minute of the day. As I reflect back, I know I was talking to

God for all of the day. A quotation I found later in my notes, with no reference as to where it came from, was "God has brought us along too far just to drop us."

Chapter 18

Retreat Day 3—Direction from God and a Letter of Anger

"Lord, here I am. I am going to listen so You can do Your work in me. I feel impatient. I want an answer to my questions, and none seems to come. What am I doing wrong? I am becoming more comfortable with silence. You are able to get me to realize that I am not silent enough. I need to learn to accept the peacefulness and beauty of silence. I can actually feel the Lord's presence. Today I do not feel the intense pain. I am beginning to feel frustration because I have been to this point before, however, and do not seem to progress. I can admit I do not know what to do or how to go deeper. I need some guidance and direction. Maybe I need to learn to pray differently. But how? I feel my patience being tested. I want an answer now, but God wants me to talk to my director, Brother Bill. Lord, I am beginning to see I am still trying to do things my way and not Your way.

"There are signs that some healing is beginning to take place. We sang 'Be Not Afraid' last night at Mass—one of the songs we sang at Tammy's funeral. Ever since her funeral, I have not been able to sing or listen to it without crying. But, last night I did. If that song had been sung on Friday night, I would have completely lost it. Is that a sign, Lord, that You are helping me to heal? I feel sad knowing that God is always available, and I have failed to take advantage of Him. I feel I have slighted myself about finding peace. Perhaps I could direct the anger at myself. I am able to forgive myself because I accept I am human and will make many mistakes. Lord, it is I who have failed You, not You who have failed me.

"Today, Brother Bill asked me to listen to God for an hour and a half. That meant sitting quietly, not journaling or reading Scripture. He wanted to see what would happen as I reflected on the new image of God I was given the day before. He suggested I leave my materials, my journal, books, and Bible in my room during this time and just be present to God.

"At first, it was hard to shut down my thoughts. I tried to concentrate on my surroundings, but that didn't last very long. After a while, trying to be completely silent and with nothing happening, I begin to get impatient. I get angry. I say, 'This is ridiculous, Lord, I know You are there, and I have some questions to be answered. I want to know what to do about going to the exact site where Tammy died. I need to know if I should try to get together with the drunk driver. What do I need to do to find peace in my heart?'"

I thought I heard a small voice inside me say, "I have been answering those questions for a while now. I need you to listen." That certainly got my attention.

"If you feel a need to go to the crash site, do not go alone. You could ask Father Con to go with you for support. Invite your family to go, but do not force them to go. They may not have the same need you do. You may need to go a few times until you can feel comfortable. You may want to call the owner of the restaurant to find out when a good time would be to go there, as you won't want to go when the place is busy." These words came as a quiet voice from within.

I had experienced these thoughts before but did not connect

them as coming from the Lord. I decided to visit the crash site when I got home. I could trust that the Lord would go with me, and I wouldn't have to do it alone.

"You may want to get in touch with the drunk driver to be able to say to him all the things you have stored up inside of you. Again, do not do this by yourself. Ask Father Con to get in touch with the drunk driver's minister to see if the two of them can come up with a time and place for all of you to meet.

"Remember when the Pope forgave the man that shot him? To find peace, you must be able to come to terms with forgiveness. You may want someone there to help mediate the feelings."

This sounded almost impossible. But I had reconciled to doing whatever it took to find inner peace.

As I was browsing through my Bible, I came across a slip of paper that referred me to Matthew 5. I began to read chapter five, verse four, "Blessed are they who mourn, for they will be comforted." This was a sign of hope for me. I knew that I would be comforted. I did not know how or when, but I trusted that comfort would come to me.

As I continued to read, three verses seemed to jump off the page at me, "Go at once and make peace with your brother, and then come back and offer your gift to God" (verse 24). Verse 44 says, "But now I tell you. Love your enemies and pray for those who persecute you so that you may become the son of your Father in heaven." And finally, verse 46, "Why should God reward you if you love only the people who love you?"

These verses seemed like they could be answers for me. To take action on any of them seemed impossible. *How could I make peace with Richard?* I did not want to have peace with him. I wanted to stay angry with him because there was no way I could let go of what he did to my daughter. The idea of loving my enemy and praying for him was just too much to ask. *How could I ever begin to pray for a drunk driver?* Yet, if I believed in Scripture, this was what

I was being asked to do. And Matthew 5:46 was not easy to look at. *Could I love those who were hard to love?* These were heavy-duty questions that I needed to reflect on for a while. I began to think that perhaps I should quit praying for answers, since the answers that were coming were not the answers I wanted. *How Lord, can I possibly do what You are asking of me? The only way I can do any of what these three verses ask of me is through Your help. Alone, I cannot do any of them.*

Now I was faced with the dilemma of to how to go about doing what these verses instructed me to do.

I was sitting outside on a bench overlooking the pond in the afternoon. I started to think about meeting with Richard and instantly grew angry. I stood up from the bench and starting walking around the pond. My pace began to pick up. All my angry thoughts were pushed forward. I began to march around the pond. I began to verbalize my anger toward the drunk driver. "I hate you for what you did to my daughter! I want you to suffer so much. I wish I knew how to hurt you in the way I have been hurt. Why should you have freedom to live your life without any daily pain? You have never cared about what you did to my family, you most inconsiderate moron. How in the world can you sleep at night knowing you killed a person?" The anger turned to rage. My words got louder and my walking was more like stomping. "Thank you, God, for pushing me around the pond and giving me physical as well as emotional release of all the anger I have felt toward that man. It seems ironic to me that I can consider forgiveness when all that anger is boiling inside me."

I don't know how many times I marched around that pond. With each step I took, I'd scream out loud my thoughts about the drunk driver and God. When I finished, I was completely exhausted. I'd needed to release the rage and fury I'd kept bottled up inside me. I'd needed it to be put into words.

I had just sat down on the bench again when the voice inside of me said, "Now go inside and write out all these angry thoughts and feelings you have harbored for so long."

As painful as that next step was, I knew I had to do it. I was beginning to trust the process the Lord was putting before me, even though I did not like having to go through all the pain once again. I have since learned that if I am obedient to what God asks me to do, peace will follow regardless of whether the task is easy or difficult.

I went back to my room and wrote the following:

Dear Richard:

It has been almost four years since you killed my daughter. I have waited every day for you to come and say, "I am sorry" and ask to be forgiven. My life has been a series of ups and downs like a roller coaster since then. I need to let you know what I have been through and all the pain you have caused my family and me.

Can you imagine what it is like hearing your daughter is dead and then finding out you can't see her to say one final goodbye? Why could I not see her? I could not see her because the car crash that you caused burned her alive. She was burned beyond recognition. Can you imagine how she must have looked? That question continues to haunt me as time goes on. Many days I question if she is even in the casket. My chance to say goodbye was snatched away because you decided to drink and then drive home.

My daughter did not deserve to die this way. She was a very good person and had many dreams and expectations for herself. She will never become the airline pilot she wanted to be, nor will she ever get married and give me grandchildren. You took care of that on September 13, 1985. I am angry. I am furious. All this could have been prevented. It need not have happened. Your irresponsibility took my daughter from me. She should still be alive today.

I was outraged when I heard the driver that killed my daughter was drunk. I consider her murdered, and the weapon was your car. She did not have a chance with that combination against her. Did you not see their car on the highway? It was a straight road with nothing in your way except your drunkenness. How could you not have stopped? Then you did not have the guts to come see my family or me and say you were sorry. What a coward you are!

I expected justice would be served with the justice system. Was I ever naive! That day in court seeing you with your attorney was another nightmare for me. You again had the opportunity to say something to our family, but no, you could not make any good come out of this tragedy. In fact, during the court process, our family was ignored, and you had all the rights. What a joke. You killed my daughter, and you have all the rights in the court process. The judge did not take the murder you committed seriously, so you got off pretty easily. No one can erase what you did from your mind. You will have to live with what you did and be accountable someday for what you did. Maybe the courts disappointed me, but God won't. Someday you will pay, and that payment will be big time.

I resent that you got to go to your job every day when you were supposed to be serving time in jail for the murder of my daughter. I hope the people you worked with scorned you. You should not have been given that right. Serving time only evenings and weekends was not enough for what you did to me by taking my precious first-born daughter from me.

My life has been in complete shambles since the death of Tammy. Yes, Tammy has a name and a face. I hope you never forget that. I was not able to function for months. My time was spent crying and grieving for the daughter you took from me. I missed work with Gene while I was attending school, I could not concentrate, and I had no memory. I thought I was going crazy. Was your night of drinking worth all the pain it has caused?

My grades in school suffered because I was no longer able to study. I could not be a mother to my other kids or be a wife to my husband in the ways I wanted. I could only stare into space or cry in despair. Do you care? I think not. Your actions say you did not care one bit about what you did.

I have been so angry with you. I wanted to burn your house down and have your kids burn up like Tammy did. Maybe it will take that before you can realize what pain I have suffered.

Not a single day goes by that I don't recall the crash and what happened. I have not been able to go out to the crash site since 1985. You took my freedom away from me too. I cannot believe you can be so inconsiderate as to not want to reach out in some way. Oh yes, I recall that at six months after the crash your wife sent a sympathy card. It was not from her that I needed a card, so I sent it back. Even then, you did not have the guts to send the card back. You have had so many opportunities to reach out, and you have not done anything.

I had so much anger I could not keep it under control. I began a chapter of Mothers Against Drunk Driving in our county.

Why? So I can take ridicule from the folks that drink and cold shoulders from the justice system. I put up with that so I can save others from going through this unbearable, excruciating pain. What have you done to try to stop drunk driving? The judge suggested you do some speaking, but it seems to me you took the easy way out, and that is to do nothing.

Well, let me tell you, I am going to be around a long time and will not let you forget what you did to Tammy. She was a beautiful, 17-year-old that had her life stolen in a most violent way. Her body was left charred black. Can you be proud of what you did to her? Can you picture her at night when you try to sleep?

Sleep is something I went without for many months. Do you care? I think not. Probably something you cannot relate to.

Yes, I am still angry with you for what has happened. I am praying hard to find a way to let go of this anger and to forgive. I have to put this in God's hands, as it is too much for me to bear anymore. Faith will show me the way, even though I don't understand. It is not an easy task, but I am struggling with it. Someday I will be in control of my emotions and myself, and it will be no thanks to you. A measly little, "I'm sorry" from you would have made such a big difference in the grieving process. But no, you were too small of a person to take responsibility for what you did. I hope you pay the price over and over for what you stole from my family and me. You stole my precious daughter's life who had her whole life in front of her. How do you handle all that, and what do you say to your kids? Do you say that their father is a murderer? They will have to live with what you did also.

—*Pat Bluth*

Chapter 19

Retreat Day 4— Hopelessness and Waiting

"Today I think I have experienced every emotion possible. The emotion I am struggling with today is loneliness for my family. I miss them so much. I wonder what they are doing and how they are getting along. It would have been easy to pack up and go home this morning.

"For three hours today on and off, I have been crying. Why can't there be an end to the crying? I do not know. It is one of those days when I feel like I am going crazy. I cannot stand to be in my room. I feel like the walls are closing in on me. What are you saying to me, Lord?

"This pain all started at 7:30 in the morning when I went to get a cup of coffee. I sat on a sofa and looked at a painting on the wall. It was Mother Mary holding baby Jesus. They both have such sad, desperate looks to their eyes. I could only think of the pain of a mother losing her child. The pain became overwhelming. I wanted to stare at it and ask why is that painting so sad looking? I had to leave and go back to my room. The pain was too intense. I did not want anyone to see me fall apart. I am still trying to figure out what all this means. The tears keep coming with no explanations. Just tears of pain. This is pain that I thought I had dealt with many times. The pain can still be as intense today as it was almost four years ago.

"Now I am again thinking about going home. I want to run away from this pain. There is nowhere to go. Just silence and more pain. I looked forward to this retreat. I am really confused. I wonder if each day will be filled with painful memories and no peace. Oh, how I want to run home to a safe place.

"I just want to be held so I can settle down. If I were home, I could ask my husband to hold me. Whom can I ask here? I know I can ask the Lord, but He feels so far away. I feel as if I am in a vacuum. No one cares about each other. Everyone here seems to be at peace but me. When will this end? Right now, I feel hopeless that this cycle will end. I can handle pain if I know it will get better, but each day it seems to get worse. I have been through hell, beyond it, and back again. I want to get off the merry-go-round. Lord, I feel You are my only way to break the cycle. How do I reach out to You and let You be there for me? How do I shut this process down? Won't You please help me?"

I spent time with my director. I read him my angry letter to Richard. Brother Bill listened intently. He did not judge me for what I had written and read to him. We sat in silence for a while. I knew he was searching for what to do next. He then gave me the task of asking Jesus to help me rewrite the letter and to see what happened.

I left with a plan, but I didn't know how to go about it. I turned to the Lord and asked Him if He would help me rewrite the letter. I heard nothing for the rest of the day. I walked. I swam. I listened. I read Scripture. I waited. Nothing came. My mind stayed silent. I wondered, *What next? How long would I have to wait?* I began to get anxious, as I knew I was halfway done with my retreat. So far, I'd only felt miserable with pain, and I didn't have much hope that anything would change. Then I thought, *Oh, you of little faith. The Lord will answer on His terms and in His time frame. I do not do well with waiting.*

Chapter 20

Retreat Day 5— Letter of Forgiveness

The Lord will speak at what could be considered the most inopportune times, but I needed to be ready to listen whenever He was ready to speak. I woke up thinking about Richard at 5:00 the next morning. I didn't like what I was hearing. I knew I should get up and begin writing out my thoughts, but I fought it. "Lord, I cannot do what You are asking of me. I cannot put these words I am hearing on a piece of paper." I had to have a talk with myself. "This is the answer you have been seeking. You asked the Lord to help you, and now you have been given the answer. Trust the process and do not let your head rule over your heart. Put the words on a piece of paper, knowing this is what the Lord is asking of you. You have come too far to let the Lord drop you now."

I began to think I was too tired to get up and write. I realize I was fighting the answers I'd been given. "What a brat I can be!" I prayed. The Lord answered, and I thought what He had to say was too burdensome to accept. I begin thinking about how the drunk driver must have suffered. I had never thought about how he had suffered before. I didn't really care if he'd suffered or not; in fact, I wanted to be sure he suffered more. I thought about getting together with him and working things out. "Stop! Stop! Lord, this is not my wish. I cannot possibly take this next step you are asking of me," I argued out loud. The Lord finally won out. I slid out of bed and wrote:

Dear Richard,
I am sure the past three plus years have not been easy on you. I think it is time we get together to reconcile our differences.

I have harbored lots of anger and resentment towards you these past years. It has done me no good but has belabored my grief. I was disappointed that you did not follow through over three years ago when you were planning a visit with our families and our pastors. I resent having to initiate the process but know it must be done.

I have lived in much pain and grief over losing Tammy. I feel like Job from the Bible. I am being punished for what I did not do. I do not understand how God works, but I know I do not have His power. I can only have faith that He understands what and why He does things.

I have thought about letting you know all the pain I have experienced. I may still have to do that. I know nothing that I say or do will bring Tammy back, and I know she is with the Lord safe and sound.

Am I trying to dump my anger on you as a sign of revenge? I guess I have wanted you to feel like I have felt. That is unreal, as I do not think you could feel like I have. After all, it was not your daughter who died.

I have never hated you, because I never had a chance to meet you or know you. I hope we get that chance soon. I need it for myself to bring a final closure to my grieving process and to let go of my pain. It will not change the fact that Tammy died, and you were responsible. I am hoping it will help me let go of four years of anger and resentment. Pope John was our model for forgiveness when he forgave the man who shot him. This is by far the hardest move of my life, but I am ready to forgive and get on.

I know that when we meet, the anger I feel toward you will want to surface. Do not be afraid of it. Let me have a chance to express it. I know I could not meet with you alone. It would be too difficult. I will need someone along for support and will be asking my priest to come also. You can bring whomever you need.

If it were up to me, I probably would not choose to forgive you. I put this process in God's hands, and He wants me to forgive. I follow what He asks of me. I forgive you.

—Pat Bluth

After writing out that letter, I was completely overwhelmed and sat down to weep. The crying was different this time. The tears were not triggered by pain but from the realization of how much the Lord loved me. He did want complete peace for me.

Later that morning as I made my bed, I looked on the floor and found a small piece of paper. On it was written, "Even if I go through the deepest darkness, I will not be afraid, O God, for you are with me" (Psalm 23:4). I wondered where the paper came from. I had no idea. I needed to learn to trust and not to seek an explanation of why God works the way He does.

A sense of overwhelming peace came over me, a peace I had

not felt for a very long time. Sharing with my director what had just happened was very exciting to me. A miracle had taken place, and I wasn't sure I understood the meaning of what it was. I needed some time to reflect on the process of forgiveness that I'd just experienced.

I was able to forgive because I let Jesus work within me. I had to forgive, or I would have lost myself. After forgiving, I felt free. A heavy burden was lifted from my shoulders. The negativity, anger, bitterness, and rage within me was released. Gone. It was no more. It was unbelievable what Jesus did for me! My heart and attitude had been changed. To feel so free was a blessing from the Lord.

I was filled with joy and excess energy throughout the day. Nothing I did was able to quiet my spirit. I walked, ran, jumped, and skipped through the whole day to use up the energy that was bursting out of me. It was weird—I'd prayed for the Lord to quiet me down, yet the opposite seemed to have happened that day. I felt almost giddy. I suppose I should have appreciated feeling that energized, but it seemed so weird; after all, I'd felt only sadness, depression, and grief for almost four years. I had forgotten what goodness actually felt like. To have such peace now was worth all the pain I had experienced.

"When you forgive, you in no way change the past—but you sure do change the future" (Bernard Meltzer).

Chapter 21

Retreat Day 6—Close to God

"Today I am feeling especially grateful to the Lord and full of love for Him. I went for a long walk and reflected on what has happened to me in the past few days. I want to savor every moment of joyfulness I feel. To celebrate that specialness, I want to curl up in God's lap and just be with Him. I have not felt this close to the Lord in years. After walking, I relaxed by the pool. Then I got my journal to express my thoughts to God in writing.

"Thank you, Lord, for allowing me to experience again these strong positive feelings. Thank you for taking my anger, bitterness, and resentment and replacing them with love. I want to run. I want to jump. I want to dance. I just want to be crazy. I want to just be. It is so special knowing this joyful part of me has not died. Lord, You knew it was there all along. You gave me the gift of persistence so I would not give up. I believe You were not going to let me surrender to grief. You wanted that special part of me to have a chance to come alive.

"I feel Your gentle presence with me as I write. I feel more at peace than I have for a long time. I know, Lord, I did it to myself. I let anger rule over love. How wonderful that You have given me another chance to redeem myself. It is Your unending forgiveness and love that keeps coming forward. I am sorry I put up roadblocks to the forgiveness process. Thank You for staying with me to tear down those walls of anger and bitterness. I know You have been at work within me. I know You will not abandon me. I know You are quieting me down. Thank You for Your gentle way.

"Help me, Lord, not to run my life but to let You be in charge of me. That is what I desire from you, Lord; that is when I find peace. I do love You, Lord, even when I am running away from You.

"I feel sadness now, knowing what I have lost. I not only lost Tammy, but a part of me died also. But now what was dead in me has come alive. Tammy has come alive in me through her spirit. We were both reborn into God's love. The sadness comes because I know I had all this love available and chose not to see that or appreciate it. The grief was just too intense.

"Timing was the key to getting to this point. Your timing was perfect, as I would not have been able to achieve this forgiveness at an earlier stage in my grieving. I would not have been ready. God, I am experiencing Your love at a much deeper level today. I know I will not always feel this way, but I am grateful for today. Please help me, Lord, not to make bad choices over You again. You are with me. Thank you, Lord, for the blessing You have given me this week. Every ounce of pain I experienced was worth it for the joy that I am feeling now."

Chapter 22

Retreat Day 7— God Answers Prayers

"I look the same, but I don't feel the same. My body is filled with so much positive energy. How am I going to take what I have learned and put it into practice? How can I find a focus for this energy? It is new to have this overabundance of energy and not have an outlet for it.

"Starting on Sunday, I sat on the bench overlooking the pond and connected with all the anger and pain I was feeling inside. Returning to the same bench today and experiencing joy and energy was a great gift from the Lord. I now feel as if I have come full circle.

"Being able to imagine I was leaning into Your lap on the bench shows me how far I have come this week. I recall that Brother Bill suggested this exercise to me on Friday evening, but I could not allow the experience to happen. Today, I could not get enough of just being in the lap of the Lord. It felt good to be able to spend time with You alone on the bench. I felt You holding me in Your arms, and I could relax. I felt so trusting and peaceful. Thank you, Lord, for bringing me this far in only a few days' time. You are very powerful in what You allow to happen.

"As I think about going home, I am scared. Will this goodness last, or will it fall apart when I get home? How will I react to others? How will they react to me? Will anyone notice any difference in me? Will anyone notice that I am not filled with anger and bitterness? But most importantly, will this last?

"As I have worked through my pain, hatred, and grief to a point of forgiveness, another thing is beginning to happen to me. The pain in my hands is improving tremendously. I hardly notice the aches and pains of arthritis anymore. The swelling is going down, and I can begin to make a fist with my hand. Thank you, Lord. I am trying to hear Your message regarding the changes in my hands. Were you trying to tell me I could not get a grip on life anymore? Is that what You were saying? Was the arthritis a way of getting my attention? Were you trying to get me to recognize how deep my pain was and that I was not letting go of it when I thought I had? Thanks for taking the pain away and restoring the use of my hands. I hope they continue to improve as I continue my growth.

"I am feeling anxious about having a face-to-face meeting with Richard. Even if there is no face-to-face meeting, I know I have still forgiven him. I feel I already have forgiven him. I somehow have the need to formalize the forgiveness process by letting him know personally. You lead, Lord, and I will follow. If roadblocks arise, I will be patient and learn to wait on You and Your timing.

"I hope my family does not think I have become some 'holy' person to whom they cannot relate. I wonder what their response will be when I share with them how I have forgiven the drunk driver and am no longer filled with anger and bitterness. They may think I have gone over the edge. I will not worry so much about what they think but will keep reflecting on what has happened to me.

"The experiences I have been through these past seven days are so overwhelming. I will need to take this day slowly to relive all I have been through.

"Yesterday I was thinking how good a rub-down would feel

just to help relax my body. It was announced at Mass that a massage therapist would be available the next day for a limited number of people. The massage would be for an hour, and there would be a small fee. I was overwhelmed with the possibility of having another prayer answered. By the time I got to the sign-up sheet for massage, there was one space available for me. The thought of how the Lord works in so many ways—big and small— became more apparent to me each time another experience was given to me. What have I done to deserve one miracle after another?"

Evening of Day 7
"Lord, I am not worthy of all that has happened this week. Every need I had and asked for was met by You. I needed to share the anger and resentment I had toward You and the driver who was responsible for Tammy's death. I was able to own all my feelings even though the anger had turned to rage and bitterness.

"With your presence, Jesus, I was able to leave four years of pain behind. I recognized I had the need to forgive God and forgive the drunk driver. In my heart, I have been able to do both. I feel that a heavy burden has been lifted from my shoulders.

"After releasing all those feelings of anger, rage, resentment, and bitterness, I then had room for God's love. I became energized. My body longed to be held and to be touched. Lord, You knew my need and you sent Sister Margaret to fulfill that need with her wonderful soothing massage.

"At the beginning of the week, Brother Bill was just what I needed. My judgment of him the first night was totally wrong. You, Lord, knew that I needed someone big and strong that could withstand all my anger and not be afraid of it. Brother Bill was there for me. He walked with me through my rough journey to peace. He withstood all my anger and rage and unconditionally accepted me and my feelings. I felt complete trust with him. I was able to be open and honest with whatever I needed to share. I held nothing back. Even though I found some things painful to talk about, Brother Bill was patient and gave me the time I needed. I knew I could take a risk, and he would be there to listen—just listen—not give me advice or answers. I was able to express my deepest feelings because of Brother Bill's ability to be there unconditionally.

"As I think about leaving this retreat tomorrow, I feel a bit apprehensive. My energy needs to be refocused so I can calm down and not begin to worry. I focus on what I am going to do differently when I get home. How will I change my behavior?

"I have such mixed emotions. I look forward to going home as I really miss my family. On the other hand, I do not want to lose the peace I have now and do not want to be let down from what I have experienced this week. I will think of Brother Bill and Jesus as surrounding me with their big arms. Then how can I go wrong?

"I am in awe of what has transpired in such a short time. Even though I have been at Dunrovin only seven days, it seems like a lot longer. Thank you, Lord, for the privilege of getting to know You through these beautiful surroundings at Dunrovin. I have felt Your presence in so many ways. I am truly grateful for being consumed by Your love. I will cherish these days forever.

"Thank You for Your gift of forgiveness. Without my acceptance of this gift from you, Lord, I would not have been able to experience Your love so deeply.

"Thank You for Your gift of compassion, caring, and trust. I felt all three very deeply. You are such a wonderful God. I am overjoyed at having this chance to know Your compassion.

"Thank You for Your gift of patience. You never gave up on me even though I gave you reason to. You were always there by my side. It must have hurt You deeply when I rejected Your love. I am glad You have forgiven me for abandoning You so many times.

"Thank You for the gift of prayer. Reading your Word in the Scripture has taught me how You want me to live. Our conversations have shown me what You want me to do. I feel special and honored that I am able to talk and share myself with You. Thank You for being my friend.

"Thank You for the gift of silence. The chance to quiet myself down and to feel Your presence has been most overwhelming. I never thought I could survive eight days of silence. I am finding out how special silence can be, and I do not want it to end. Silence is what I need to be able to get in touch with my inner being—the real me that You love so deeply.

"Thank You for the opportunity and privilege to be on this retreat. Thanks for making it possible for me to be here. Thank You for Father Con, for his listening to my pain, and for knowing what I needed to do to get closer to You. Thanks to my family for taking charge of the responsibilities at home and giving me the support to be away on retreat. Thank You for the Loyola staff who made the retreat possible.

"Thank You for my director, Brother Bill. He was just what I needed. He was full of compassion, patience, and unconditional love. What an example of you, Lord. You knew all along what it was I needed and placed Brother Bill before me.

"I feel loved and special. My heart wants to burst with fullness, warmth, and love. Thank You, Lord, for making me the woman I am and for leading me to You.

"Thank You, Lord, for my pain. It was through my pain that I was given the opportunity to grow deeper in love."

Chapter 23

Retreat Day 8—Peace at Last

Since this retreat would end after lunch, I only had time to meet with Brother Bill for 30 minutes. That time would be used to say goodbye and to set a goal as to how I could keep what I had learned during the retreat active and moving.

After sharing with Brother Bill what I had written the day before in appreciation to God for all that had transpired this week, I told him how much I appreciated his presence and compassion. He told me he had only been asked to be a director just days before the retreat began. I knew he was in God's plan for me. He said he was in awe himself after witnessing how God healed my pain through forgiveness. Brother Bill said he planned to go to the library to do some research on grieving parents who had lost a child. Before meeting me, he had not experienced being around someone with so much pain and anger. He felt privileged to be a part of my healing and was thankful to God. He suggested I set some goals to keep connected with God on a daily basis.

Mass was scheduled at 10:00, and following it each person on retreat would be given an opportunity to share their experience. How could I share my experience in just a few short statements? That would be a challenge after all that had happened during the week.

When it came to my turn I said, "I came to this retreat filled with anger, bitterness, rage, and an unforgiving heart. My 17-year-old daughter was killed on September 13, 1985 by a drunk driver. The pain of her death consumed my every moment for the past three and a half years. I leave this retreat with my anger, resentment, bitterness, and rage stomped into the ground around the pond. I leave with a heart filled with love, joy, and peace. I have been able to forgive the drunk driver. I have experienced one of God's miracles."

"Never forget the three powerful resources you always have available to you: love, prayer, and forgiveness" (H. Jackson Brown, Jr.).

Chapter 24

What Can Be Learned About Mourning

Grieving is a process that takes work that is unique for each person. No two people will deal with mourning in the same way. At the beginning, most people deal with many common symptoms. Some of these are difficulty concentrating, forgetfulness, restlessness, sadness, fearfulness, lack of energy, exhaustion, fatigue, overeating or loss of appetite, insomnia, bad dreams, anger, guilt, anxiety, fear, change in sexual desire, increased drinking, suicidal thoughts, feeling of powerlessness over life, helplessness, and loneliness. This is not an all-inclusive list. You may experience all of these symptoms or you may not. If you do not experience most of these symptoms, that does not mean that there is anything wrong with you. Don't invent issues if they are not there. One woman in a grief group was relieved after hearing a list of common symptoms. She said, "I am so relieved that what I am feeling is normal. I thought there was something wrong with me."

Grieving is understood more by your experience than from anything else. The pain and anguish one feels is difficult to describe to others in order for them to understand completely. Experience is the best teacher, and that saying also holds true while dealing with grief. My personal experience with grief before the death of my daughter was pretty limited. Except for what I'd read in books, I had not much to fall back on for help. What I read in books or had studied in school did not prepare me adequately for understanding the depth of the pain I experienced after Tammy died. The pain gripped me from my head to my toes until my whole body ached. I craved the opportunity to hold my daughter one more time. My arms often had a steady aching that lasted for hours. I learned that the aching in my arms was my yearning to hug my daughter, to hold her once again.

Of course, tears are a normal aspect to grieving. Don't be afraid of your tears. Many, including me, fear that their crying will continue for a lifetime. I can assure you that the tears will end; I can't tell you exactly when they will end. Tears became a common companion to me. I thought I would never see an end to tears. At times I wondered how there could possibly be any more tears inside of me. Crying would go on for hours and days at a time. I'd cry over most anything. Anything that reminded me of Tammy stirred up the emptiness I felt inside and resulted in a flood of tears. My family didn't know how to handle me. There was not anything at that point that could have made me feel any better.

I actually thought I'd feel like that the rest of my life. I couldn't imagine that there'd ever be another happy day in my life. A huge part of me had died inside, and I couldn't bring that part of me to life again. Tammy was my firstborn. I should have been able to protect her. I should have been able to see her graduate from high school, from college, get married, have children, and have a long life. Then suddenly everything was thrown off. I had no security that I would outlive my other children.

My body felt like a robot in motion but without emotions. It was not unusual for me to get up and sit in a chair and stare into space. The emptiness was so intense. The only feeling I could associate with was despair. Tammy was constantly on my mind. I thought of her 24 hours a day. I couldn't get her out of my mind. I tried to relive the past days, months, and years. I was afraid I'd forget how she looked and how her voice sounded. I wanted to recall all our conversations. Had I told her I loved her enough? Did she think of me as she was dying?

Grieving is not something that anyone can do for you. Even though I had friends and family who were supportive, nothing they said or did could take the pain away. There are no easy answers to grieving.

As I reflect back on how our family grieved, the process was so different for each of us. I was one who needed to cry openly, and I did, no matter where I was.

Paranoia is typical when grieving in thinking that you have now become the center of attention. About two days after the funeral, I had to go to the grocery store for a few items. I could sense others' discomfort when they passed me in the aisle. I know some went out of their way to avoid me. Others gathered together, and I could tell they were discussing me as I walked by. I felt like everyone in the store was staring at me. It was a most unpleasant experience.

Hardly a day went by without someone asking, "How are you doing?" That became a question I began to dread hearing. It also became apparent that people who asked the question did not really want to hear how I was doing. I got to the point when others would ask me how I was doing, I wanted to scream, "Do you really care?" I had to find an answer to that question. "Fine" was the response they expected. When I was not fine, I wasn't sure that anyone cared to hear the truth. Few who asked how I was doing really wanted the truthful answer. Many people would walk away as they were asking the question. It was like the saying, "Have a good day." Do people really care if you have a good day? Do they want a report the next day on how your day went? I think not. It is similar in grief. It becomes a trite question that the person grieving begins to resent hearing unless the person asking the question actually wants to take the time to hear the answer. You begin to discern who really cares about how you're doing from those who just ask but don't want the answer. I don't think I will lose the need to talk about the death of Tammy.

It felt good to talk, talk, and talk some more. I needed to tell my story over and over again, but it was difficult to find people who were willing to listen to my story over and over again.

My husband, Gary, wanted to keep his grief inside himself. He got more involved in his job to work through his grief in a way totally different from mine. When I shared my tears and anger with him, he'd listen graciously, but then he'd try to "fix" me. By giving me advice that I didn't need or want, he often added to the pain and frustration I was experiencing. Also, when I shared my grief, it would get Gary in touch with his grief. Most of the time, this would leave us both worn out and emotionally exhausted.

Grief puts a tremendous strain on a marriage. We had a good marriage before Tammy's death. If our marriage had been rocky or insecure, I really doubt we would have made it through the following years together. Our commitment to the marriage was what helped us get through the rough times. We had limited energy for each other to offer support. Many days we would exist in the same house with hardly any emotional connection, as we were both in so much individual pain that we had nothing to give to each other. I would nag him to talk, and he would respond with, "I have nothing to say." For me, talking was my way to handle grief. I couldn't understand why Gary wouldn't talk about how he felt. I'd get so angry with him for how he was handling his mourning. It was very hard for me to back off and to allow him to grieve in his own way. Giving him my good advice did not work any better than my trying to take his advice.

What helped me to let go was hearing a statistic that 70 percent of parents whose child dies end up divorced. I had already become one statistic—a victim of drunk driving—and knew I did not want to become another.

After letting go of nagging Gary to talk, I began to lean on my friends more to do my grieving and sharing. By doing this, it took the pressure off my husband and it gave me some energy to be able to support him. This seems to have worked, as twenty-one years later we have not become another divorce statistic.

Forgetfulness is a common characteristic of grief. I would go to the store, write out a check, and put my checkbook back into my purse without tearing out the check. I would set the table for five of us when there were now only four. I could be in the middle of a thought or sentence and not remember what I was talking about. I would go to another room to get something only to realize I had forgotten why I went there. Thoughts left me as fast as they arrived. Before Tammy's death, I often filled spare time by reading; now I found it almost impossible to remember what I'd read from sentence to sentence. This added to the frustration I already felt over so many other things. Reading books was too overwhelming a task to take on at the beginning of my mourning.

Restlessness became familiar to me. If I sat still too long or if there was silence, I would begin to think about Tammy, and the pain would rush in to hurt me.

When Tammy died, I was attending Saint Cloud State University working on my Masters Degree in Counseling. The first day of new classes, shortly after the funeral, each person had to give his or her name and tell something about himself or herself. I got through saying my name, but then I began to cry. No one knew that I had just buried my daughter, so it seemed odd that I would be crying at such an easy assignment. I could not complete the simple assignment of verbally stating something about myself. The class I was taking was small group counseling. It became a means for me to share my grief with others studying to be counselors. Each class became easier to attend, and in May, 1987, I received my Masters Degree in Community Counseling. Grieving did not keep me from meeting my goal; quitting had not been an option.

Many times the grief I suffered would be because of Tammy's missed opportunities since she died so young. Following the party I'd had for Tammy's posthumous 18th birthday, when no one mentioned her name, many others said to me that they wished I had brought up Tammy's name. I learned from that experience that it was important for me to take the lead in talking about my daughter. Others looked to me for guidance for what to do. Sometimes what we learn can only come from our experience. If I had to do it over again, I would have had photo albums out with pictures of Tammy and her friends and family. I would have had each person tell us something they remembered about her. I think that would have been a good plan for all of us. It was a learning experience.

Grief is a long process that consists of daily work. Tears, anger, guilt, questions, answers, no answers, all begin to become a daily part of life. Time helps to lessen all that, but it does not completely eliminate it. Mourning is a lifetime commitment that does not have to control you or consume you. I learned to take it as it came and not to have overly high expectations for myself, especially during the first year.

When I began to have some good moments, some good days, something would come along that would set me back to square one again. I'd hear a song, find a piece of Tammy's clothing, read something in the newspaper, see something on television, or something else that would trigger the grief and remind me that Tammy had died.

Some of the following statements were common in the grief groups I facilitated:

- "I cannot stand being alone."
- "I don't think I will ever find happiness again."

- "I feel so lonely, and I can't reach out to others."
- "My life and time seems so wasted."
- "I can't accomplish anything."
- "I should be feeling better by now."
- "I have no interest in anything now."
- "I wonder if I will be like this forever."

I offer reassurance that these thoughts are normal. What a person feels in the early stages of grief will not last for a lifetime. With time and work, the feelings will gradually dissipate. What I can't tell a person is how long those feelings will last. Most people want to know when they will feel better. That is not an easy question to answer, as grief is so unique to each person.

The following may be helpful suggestions for you to follow when you are mourning:

- At times we all need some help, so do not be afraid to ask for it and accept it.
- Make your needs known to others by expressing them, rather than putting on a brave front.
- Being severely upset is not unusual at the beginning of the grieving process. It is always good to seek advice from a doctor if you are concerned that your experience is out of the ordinary.
- There is no time limit for grieving. Be gentle with yourself, and give yourself ample time for it.
- Isolation is not always healthy. If you need company, or someone to talk with, let it be known to your friends or family. You will not always be dependent on others.
- Take care of yourself by eating regularly. Look at food as your medicine to survive and give you the added energy you need.
- Because you are under so much stress, you may be more susceptible to illness. See your doctor if you have any concerns.
- Even though you may not be able to sleep without some disturbance, you can at least get rest.

• During the early stages of grieving, friends and family are available for support. After some time, they will be less available. You will need to reach out to them, but don't expect them to read your mind. They will usually not be able to do so.

• No one will be able to replace your loss, but other people can help fill the gap. Try to meet new friends and enjoy their company and support.

• Express your feelings. There is no need to hide or mask what you are feeling.

• Let your faith be a major part of your healing. God can handle your feelings, both positive and negative. He is already aware of your feelings, so talk them through with Him. Maintaining your spiritual life may be difficult while in the throes of abject despair, but don't let go of it; use it to work through the difficulty you may be having.

• Be gentle with yourself while grieving. Be gentle with yourself while grieving. This cannot be stressed enough.

There are many statements that people will say to you that may not help you feel better. Some of those statements may be more hurtful than helpful. The following are some examples of what might be said to a parent who has just lost a child:

• "You can have other children."
• "You are lucky you had her/him for this many years."
• "Now you don't have to see them suffer."
• "Fake it, until you make it."
• "You still have other children."
• "God must have wanted your daughter/son in heaven."

These may be well-intentioned statements, and they may be true statements; however, none of them are comforting when a parent is heartbroken over the loss of their beloved child.

The goal of grieving is to be able to get to the point where you can accept the fact that you have just experienced a major loss in your life. This does not mean forgetting the loss happened. I see acceptance as taking control of your grief rather than letting grief control you. It is now time to learn to live with your suffering and know you can handle your problems each day. You can begin to live each day with some bits of happiness. There can be a purpose to your living again. Try to focus on what you still have in your life and not so much on what you have lost. Be gentle with yourself and give yourself plenty of time to grieve. Remember that society may give you three to six months to grieve, but, in reality, your mourning will be with you a lifetime. But you can be in charge of your grief.

I often wished mourning would be like reading a good book—there is a start and a finish. When I finish reading a book, I can slam it shut and never have to think about it again. I can put it on a shelf and say, "I am finished." Grief, however, continues to be triggered and does not have an ending where today I could say, "I am finished."

Chapter 25

Helping Other Victims

In the past 21 years, I have worked diligently with many victims so they will have a chance to be heard and have their rights made known. The most important role for me as an advocate when working with victims is to listen and hear what the victim has to say and to remember that I am the voice of the victim. That means I must be able to advocate for what the victim wants, not necessarily what I want. The two may be different and at times have been very different. I may want a very tough sentence when the victim wants only an apology and nothing else.

My first goal as an advocate is to hear the victim's story. This gives them a chance to tell his or her story and gives me an opportunity to know what I need to do when working with that individual. Some victims can be more assertive and can contact the necessary departments, and with some victims I need to do this for them. Some victims already have copies of accident reports and know what has happened; others may not have much information. Then, I know I need to refer them to the proper authorities to get information regarding their loved one's crash. After listening to them, I can understand the victims' needs. Many times victims have misconceptions as to what to expect during the court procedures. Many often think there will be a long, involved trial that will take place when the first court date is scheduled. If and when there is a trial, it could take place months from the beginning court date. In fact, many cases are settled without going to trial. Only one case that I have advocated for has actually gone to trial. Victims don't understand this, so from the very beginning I know I have a lot of work to do to explain how the courts work.

Realizing that the court process can take several months from start to finish is not easy for victims to handle. There are many delays, postponements, and court schedules around which to work. The victim often does not want to hear that, as their only concern is receiving justice. Victims don't understand why the defendants don't just plead guilty when they know they are guilty. I clarify to them that I am not an attorney, so I will explain the court system in laymen's terms. It is a simplified version, but one that victims can understand.

The first court date to be set is known as an arraignment. The defendant appears before the judge and is informed of the charges. The defendants are informed of their rights. The defendant can respond to the charges. The defendant can be assigned a public defender if necessary. The victim has no rights at the arraignment except being able to be in the courtroom if they choose. This whole process takes only a few minutes. The defendant is usually allowed to go home with some restrictions given by the courts.

Another court date is then set for an omnibus hearing. This court date may be held two or three months later, depending on the court calendar. The purpose of an omnibus hearing is to see whether there is enough evidence to support the charges. The defense side can attack the evidence. It is important for the victim to have the prosecuting attorney explain to them the strengths and weaknesses of the case. In addition, the victim often has additional information that may be helpful to the prosecuting attorney. The judge may also need to have some time to look over the information that is presented at the omnibus hearing. If so, another court date will be scheduled to allow the judge to present his findings. The defense side may waive the omnibus hearing and can plead guilty or not guilty at that time.

If the defendant pleads guilty, a court date is set for sentencing. If the defendant pleads not guilty, a court date is set for a trial. Again, this date will be months away because of the court calendar. At any time before the trial, the defendant can change his or her plea to guilty. In that case, there would be no trial but a date set for sentencing. When a court date is set, the date may be changed for many reasons. The defense attorney may not have had enough time to review the case, information was not available, witnesses may not be available, people can get sick, or they can even be having surgery. Each of these reasons could cause the date to be changed. There could also be plea negotiating going on between the prosecuting attorney and the defense attorney. If the defendant pleads guilty to the crime charged or to a lesser crime, they will try to reach an agreement regarding sentencing. This agreement then has to be presented before the judge for approval. However, victims should be notified and talked to about these negotiations. Victims have a right to have input in the plea-bargaining negotiations.

At the time of sentencing, victims have a right to present a victim-impact statement. The victim has the right to speak in court telling how the crash has affected the family. The victim then becomes known to the courts. A face is put to a case number. The victim becomes real to all involved in the court process. The victim-impact statement should be short—about three to five minutes, and should express the physical, financial, and emotional loss the crash has caused the family. This is an opportunity to let the courts know what kind of person the victim was and how the victim's family has been affected. The statement can also give an opinion regarding sentencing. One creative sentence a judge agreed to was having the defendant place a rose at the crash site on each anniversary date of the crash for 14 years. Request for restitution for out-of-pocket expenses can be included in the statement.

This statement is then read aloud in the courtroom. I have stood up several times in the courtroom as an advocate with the victim by my side and read the statement for the victim. It is important that the statement be read for all to hear. The statements have made a difference. After listening to the statement in the courtroom on one particular case, the judge said he was giving a stiffer sentence based on what he had learned from the victim reading their statement. Without the statement being read, the judge would not have any idea of the extent of the injuries to the victims. The only charge that could be given in that case was a DWI, since the injuries the victim received were not permanent. If the injuries of victims are permanent, then a different charge with a stiffer sentence can be given. In this case, the victim-impact statement was the only opportunity for the judge to learn of the victim's injuries and hear how the crash had affected him or her.

Many times the victim may not like the outcome of the case, but they usually feel good about their involvement in it. When victims are part of the court process, they will be less likely to feel victimized a second time. Not all drunk-driving crash victims take advantage of advocacy; many struggle throughout the court process. One prosecuting attorney told me, "I welcome victim advocates, as it makes my job easier." I wish all involved in the court system would have that attitude.

Doing something to help other victims has made me realize that something positive can come out of a tragedy. Becoming a victim's advocate and helping others through the court process has been a benefit to the victims as well as to me. Doing something positive with my anger was helpful and healing, but not the entire answer to internal peace.

Chapter 26

Forgiveness

Forgiveness for me was a process, a long, difficult, painful process. Defining forgiveness was a challenge. At first, I thought that if I forgave, then I had to forget what happened. I thought forgiveness was impossible. I knew I'd never be able to forget my daughter or what happened to her. There were many blocks to my being able to forgive Richard. I was not ready to forgive right away, as I needed to feel the anger I was experiencing. I had to give myself time to grieve. In the beginning stages of thinking about forgiveness, I could only think about what it would do for him, face to face. I was so angry with Richard that I didn't want to do anything that would make him feel better. I did not want to have to talk with him and tell him I forgave him, and then all would be well. Before I could forgive him, I wanted him to come to me. In other words, I had a condition to forgiveness. All this wrong thinking about forgiveness kept me mourning for a lot longer than necessary.

What I have learned about forgiveness is far different from my first confusing thoughts. Forgiveness is possible and is necessary to find peace. Forgiveness cannot happen to a human being without God's help. It would have been impossible for me to forgive Richard on my own. Forgiveness has nothing to do with the other person. I needed to forgive, not for him, but for myself. It did not matter what he did. Forgiveness was to free me from the anger, rage, and bitterness that controlled my life in a negative way.

Being able to say the words "I forgive you" was a decision I had to make. I could have fought God and not chosen to say those three simple words. I could have left the retreat feeling better because I processed the pain, but lasting peace in my heart would not have taken place. I believe that in my heart. Forgiveness is possible whether you have the opportunity to tell the other person or not. Forgiveness is the most freeing gift that God has given me. It was the only thing that worked for me to be at peace with my daughter's death.

The thoughts of Nancy Stark Muyskens in her book, *The Curtain Is Torn*, say a lot to me about forgiveness:

Many of us have been taught as Christians that we are to forgive. We have been told that forgiveness is a choice. As a result, we will try to muster up enough strength to say to God, "Oh, all right, I forgive." We may even try to sound earnest when we say it. We say it in hopes that those words will take away the enormous pain that goes along with unforgiveness. We learn quickly that words are not enough to rid us of the ugly trust that remains in our heart. The ugly self-destructive thoughts of unworthiness and/or the ugly residue of hatred are often the truth of what remains after we have offered to God our choice to forgive.

Forgiveness is not something we can generate within ourselves. Our natural selves are not made out of the stuff that forgiveness requires. We are naturally made out of "self stuff," not "God stuff." Our focus will turn inward, not upward. This kind of inward thinking leads us farther away from forgiveness. These

---

thoughts lead to bitterness, resentment, hopelessness, unlovability, and unforgiveness.

I am convinced that forgiveness is something that we are incapable of arriving at apart from God intervening in our lives. Forgiveness is not a choice—forgiveness is a miracle. We cannot experience freedom from the power of unforgiveness. Thankfully, God is waiting to intervene by providing a way that we can experience the miracle of forgiveness.

Forgiveness is long-lasting. My anger, rage, bitterness, is still at Dunrovin around the pond. To this day, I have never felt any of those strong feelings for Richard since being able to forgive him. Forgiveness is available to anyone who wants to take advantage of it.

I want to recap the steps I took on retreat to be able to feel free again so I can enjoy life.

• First, I had to identify and own all my thoughts and feelings. The crazy thoughts that seemed far out or even bizarre had to be claimed as mine. I had to put words to my anger, bitterness, rage, vengefulness, hopelessness, and despair.

• Second, I wrote down all the crazy thoughts that were going through my mind. I had to include my feelings and emotions not only about the drunk driver but toward God as well.

• Third, I shared all those thoughts and feelings with another person. I read aloud to my director what I had written.

• Fourth, I wrote a letter to Tammy's killer. I didn't send the letter, but I used it to describe what the anger inside me was about.

• Fifth, I prayed and asked Jesus to help me rewrite the letter I had written. I sat quietly waiting to hear the words that Jesus would give me.

• Sixth, I had to be willing to write down the words I was given from Jesus and to be able to say, "I forgive you." I had to accept the power of forgiveness that Jesus showed me.

To forgive is not a simple process. One might think so as they read the above steps, but the pain and hurt of not forgiving are worse than the pain of going through the forgiveness process.

Is there a low point in your life where you have felt the worst form of despair, anger, resentment, or rage towards another person? Towards yourself? Have you been hurt, abused, and traumatized in your life so badly that you think it will never get better? Perhaps your pain was not by the death of a child, but by some other means. Are you harboring negative feelings by holding on to anger, bitterness, or unforgiveness? Is that pain controlling you? Is your heart broken, and day after day you experience the pain eating away at your insides? Are you unable to forgive?

Then it is time for you to reach out to Jesus. Ask Him for answers to how He wants to help you. Can you apply the forgiveness process I was given to your situation? Hanging on to your anger, resentment, and bitterness has a negative affect on you and your physical health.

When we have been hurt by others, it may seem impossible to forgive. My health and peace were deteriorating when I confronted the anger, hate, bitterness, resentment, and unforgiveness without the help of Jesus. Don't let that happen to you. With the help of Jesus, forgiveness is possible in situations that seem impossible. Forgiveness will free you of your pain and past hurts.

I want you to have the peace Jesus has given to me. Take control of your hurt and pain. It is worth the pain of taking the path to finding inner peace through forgiveness. The three words I forgive you can set you free. You will find that your hurt and despair can be transformed into joy and peace. I ask you to have the courage, and to take the risk, to do what it takes to ask Jesus into your life and to help you come to terms with any unforgiving feelings you may be dealing with in your life. It is good to be free.

My life has gone from one extreme to the other, from having suicidal thoughts to being able to help others. This was a process that was only possible because of God's love.

Richard refused to meet with Father Con and myself, so I have not shared with him the fact that I have forgiven him. Even though we were not able to meet, that has not affected my forgiveness.

Arthritis is no longer a part of my life. Shortly after the retreat, I was taken off aspirin to prepare me for some tests. To everyone's surprise, no physical pain remained. Today, I am on no medication for arthritis. I was miraculously healed, both physically and emotionally.

In 1987, I earned a Masters degree in Community Counseling. I worked for 11 years as a family therapist at Christian Counseling and Reconciliation in Brainerd. This has been a gift from God. Through God, I was able to help many people who had lost hope. God works in many ways and He has shown that to me over and over.

My advocacy work with Mothers Against Drunk Driving continues to be important to my life. God has used me in many ways to reach out to others who have been affected by people driving drunk. That such good can come out of bad is truly miraculous. When working with victims, I can honestly say, "I have walked in your shoes." I understand the pain of having a loved one die in a senseless, preventable car crash. My heart goes out to others, and I can offer their pain up to God. He is the answer for lasting peace.

My spiritual life continues to soar with God's love. There are still days I abandon God and take control of my life. Sometimes I don't pray to God before making a decision, which then often turns out to be the wrong decision. I ignore my routine of reading Scripture or praying, and then I feel distant from Him. God is there quickly to remind me when I am off track. I have attended several six- to eight-day silent retreats since 1989. On my second retreat, God blessed me with Father Greg as my director. I continue to see him every other month for spiritual direction. I need him so I can stay accountable for my spiritual growth.

There are miracles waiting for you, as there were for me. Don't let them pass by. I hope you will experience the gift of peace through God's miracles.

"Nothing that is worth doing can be achieved in our lifetime; therefore we must be saved by hope. Nothing which is true or beautiful or good makes complete sense in any immediate context of history; therefore we must be saved by faith. Nothing we do, however virtuous, can be accomplished alone; therefore we must be saved by love. Forgiveness is the final form of love" (Reinhold Niebuhr).

If there are people you need to forgive, turn to God in prayer. Ask for His help. Forgiveness is possible. Forgiveness is your answer to peace in your life.

About the Author

Pat Bluth was born in Bremerton, Washington, but life brought her to Brainerd, Minnesota, where, along with her husband, Gary, they have lived and raised three children: Tammy, Jeff, and Jennifer.

Life was going well for the Bluth family, but everything changed suddenly when one Friday night, daughter Tammy was killed by a drunk driver.

For months after Tammy's death, Pat struggled to go on with life, but because of her strong faith, she persevered and has used her life experiences to help others facing life changing situations. She completed a Master's Degree in Community Counseling, and has used her abilities as an Independent Clinical Social Worker to facilitate grief groups for Home Care/Hospice at St. Joseph's Medical Center and for Compassionate Friends, listening and comforting parents who experience the death of a child. She served in private practice as a family therapist for a Christian Counseling Clinic in Brainerd, and is also certified as a Chemical Dependency Counselor.

Pat was instrumental in forming a Mothers Against Drunk Driving chapter in the Brainerd Lakes Area and is a frequent speaker at MADD impact panels. She has worked as a victim advocate for others whose lives have been shattered by impaired drivers. As a Certified Toastmaster, Pat enjoys opportunities to speak and spread a message of hope and inspiration to various audiences. She shares her story of how God turned her bitterness into forgiveness, and how it is possible to enjoy life again, even after great tragedy has occurred. Her message has inspired thousands.

A member of the Brainerd Area Catholic Churches, Pat is a Lector and a Minister of Holy Communion. She has served on boards for the Council of Catholic Women at the local, Deanery, and Diocesan levels. Because of her commitment to God and her service in church and the community, Pat has been able to use life's struggles to grow spiritually, and finds it her mission to encourage others along the way.

Contact Information

To contact the author for speaking engagements or to obtain more books, write: pat@patbluth.com or visit her on the web at www.patbluth.com.

DATE DUE

GAYLORD

PRINTED IN U.S.A.

LaVergne, TN USA
17 August 2009

155050LV00012B/112/P

9 781581 692952